OF THE POEM

MERIDIAN

Crossing Aesthetics

Werner Hamacher

& David E. Wellbery

Editors

Translated by
Daniel Heller-Roazen

Stanford
University
Press

Stanford
California

THE END
OF THE POEM

Studies in Poetics

Giorgio Agamben

The End of the Poem: Studies in Poetics
was originally published in Italian in 1996
under the title *Categorie italiane: Studi di poetica*
© 1996 by Marsilio Editori for the Italian edition

Stanford University Press
Stanford, California

© 1999 by the Board of Trustees
of the Leland Stanford Junior University

Printed in the United States of America

CIP data appear at the end of the book

Acknowledgments

"Comedy" first appeared in *Paragone* 347 (1978). "*Corn*: From Anatomy to Poetics" was published in *Le Moyen Âge dans la modernité, Mélanges offerts à Roger Dragonetti*, ed. Jean R. Scheidegger, Sabine Girardet, and Eric Hicks (Geneva: Champion, 1996). "The Dream of Language," originally written for the Fondazione Cini conference "Languages of Dreaming," appeared in *Lettere italiane* 4 (1982). "Pascoli and the Thought of the Voice" was published as a preface to Giovanni Pascoli, *Il fanciullino* (Milan: Feltrinelli, 1982). "The Dictation of Poetry" appeared as a preface to Antonio Delfini's *Poesie della fine del mondo* (Macerata: Quodlibet, 1995). "Expropriated Manner" was published as a preface to Giorgio Caproni, *Res amissa* (Milan: Garzanti, 1991). "The Celebration of the Hidden Treasure" was presented at a conference on Elsa Morante in Perugia in January 1993. "The End of the Poem" was presented November 10, 1995, at the University of Geneva during a conference honoring Roger Dragonetti. "An Enigma Concerning the Basque Woman" appeared in *Marka* 27 (1990). "The Hunt for Language" was published in *Il Manifesto*, January 23, 1990. "The Just Do Not Feed on Light" appeared in *Idra* 5 (1992) as an introduction to Eugenio De Signoribus's poems. "Taking Leave of Tragedy" was published in *Fine secolo*, December 7, 1985.

G.A.

Contents

Preface

Between 1974 and 1976 I met regularly in Paris with Italo Calvino and Claudio Rugafiori to define the program of a review. The project was ambitious, and our conversations, which often were not entirely focused, followed the dominant motifs and muffled echoes of each of our interests. We were, however, in agreement about one thing: one section of the review was to be dedicated to the definition of what we called "Italian categories." It was a matter of identifying nothing less than the categorial structures of Italian culture through a series of conjoined polar concepts. Claudio immediately suggested *architecture/vagueness* (that is, the domination of the mathematical-architectonic order alongside the perception of beauty as something vague). Italo had already been ordering images and themes along the coordinates of *speed/lightness*. Working on the essay on the title of the *Divine Comedy* that opens this collection, I proposed that we explore several oppositions: *tragedy/comedy, law/creature, biography/fable.*

For reasons that need not be clarified here, the project was never realized. Once we had returned to Italy, we all—if in different ways—confronted the political change that was already under way and that was to impress the 1980s with its dark seal. It was obviously a time not for programmatic definitions, but for resistance and flight. Echoes of our common project can be found in Italo's *American Lectures,* as well as in a large notebook that has remained among his papers. For my part, I attempted to establish the physiognomy of the project, before it was definitively canceled, in the "program for a review" published *in limine* in *Infancy and History*. (Those who are interested may look in those pages for the provisional list of categories in their original, problematic context.)

In their own way, the eight studies collected here (the first of which dates from the time of the project, the last of which was finished in 1995) remain faithful to this program. In the course of time, other categories came to be added to those rudimentary first ones (*mother tongue / grammatical language*; *living language / dead language*; *style / manner*). At the same time, the project of a definition of these categories gradually gave way to a study of the general problems in poetics that they implied. Each of the essays in this book thus seeks to define a general problem of poetics with respect to an exemplary case in the history of literature. The inquiry into the reasons for the title of Dante's *Comedy* makes it possible to cast new light on the comedy/tragedy opposition at the beginning of Romance poetry; a reading of *Hypnerotomachia Polifili* and Pascoli considers the problem of the relation between living language and dead language as a fundamental internal tension in the poetics of modernity; the introduction to the poetic work of a contemporary Italian writer, Antonio Delfini, functions as an occasion to reformulate the old problem of the relation between life and poetry and to define the principle of narrative in Romance literatures as an invention of lived experience on the basis of poetry; and, finally, an analysis of one of the greatest poets of the twentieth century, Giorgio Caproni, defines the act of writing with respect to the dialectical tension of style and manner.

In "*Corn*: From Anatomy to Poetics" and "The End of the Poem," the subject of study shifts to the problem of the specific structure of the poem itself. These two essays are thus to be understood as a first contribution to a philosophy and criticism of meter that do not yet exist. The first of these essays, which examines Arnaut Daniel's obscene *sirventes*, develops Roman Jakobson's problem of the relation between sound and sense; the second, which lends its title to the book as a whole, considers the end of the poem as a point of crisis that is in every sense fundamental to the structure of poetry.

The initial program of a systematic grid of the categories bearing on Italian culture nevertheless remains unfinished, and this book merely offers a torso of the idea of which we once tried to catch sight. It is therefore dedicated to the memory not only of companionship, but also of the one among us who is no longer present to bear witness to it.

THE END
OF THE POEM

§ 1 Comedy

I. THE PROBLEM

1. The aim of this essay is the critical assessment of an event that can be chronologically dated at the beginning of the fourteenth century but that, by virtue of its still exerting a profound influence on Italian culture, can be said to have never ceased to take place. This event is the decision of a poet to abandon his own "tragic" poetic project for a "comic" poem. This decision translates into an extremely famous *incipit*, which one of the author's letters states as follows: "Here begins the Comedy of Dante Alighieri, a Florentine by birth, not by disposition" (*Incipit comoedia Dantis Alagherii florentini natione non moribus*). The turn registered by these words is so little a question internal to Dante scholarship that it can even be said that here, for the first time, we find one of the traits that most tenaciously characterizes Italian culture: its essential pertinence to the comic sphere and consequent refutation of tragedy.

The fact that even a few years after the author's death the reasons for the comic title appeared problematic and incoherent to the oldest commentators[1] bears witness to the extent to which this turn hides a historical knot whose repression cannot easily be brought to consciousness. All the more surprising is the poverty of modern critical literature on the subject. That a scholar such as Pio Rajna (who so influenced later studies) could reach such obviously

insufficient conclusions as those with which his study of the
poem's title ends[2] is something that cannot be explained even by
Italian culture's lack of contact with its own origins. Even Erich
Auerbach, the author of such penetrating works on Dante's style,
does not succeed in explaining the poem's *incipit* in satisfying
terms. "Dante," he writes, referring to the ancient theory of the
separation of styles, "never freed himself completely from these
views; otherwise he would not have called his great work a comedy in clearest opposition to the term *alta tragedia* which he ap-
plied to Virgil's *Aeneid*."[3] And, concerning Dante's letter to Cangrande, Auerbach writes:

> It is not easy to see how Dante, after having found this formula and
> after having completed the Comedy, could still have expressed him-
> self upon its character with the pedantry exhibited in the passage from
> the letter to Cangrande just referred to. However, so great was the
> prestige of the classical tradition, obscured as it still was by pedantic
> schematization, so strong was the predilection for fixed theoretical
> classifications of a kind which we can but consider absurd, that such a
> possibility cannot be gainsaid after all.[4]

As far as explanations for Dante's choice of title are concerned, in
a certain sense modern criticism has not progressed beyond Benvenuto da Imola's observations or the suggestions with which Boccaccio ends his commentary on the title of the poem. "What,"
Boccaccio asks,

> will we then say of the objections that have been made against it? On
> the grounds that the author was a most prudent man, I believe that
> he would have had in mind not the parts contained in comedy but its
> entirety, and that he named his book on the basis of this entirety, so
> to speak. And from what one can infer from Plautus and Terence, who
> were comic poets, the entirety of comedy is this: comedy has a turbu-
> lent principle, is full of noise and discord, and ends finally in peace
> and tranquillity. The present book altogether conforms to this model.
> Thus the author begins with woes and infernal troubles and ends it in
> the peace and glory enjoyed by the blessed in their eternal life. And
> this certainly suffices to explain how the said title suits this book.[5]

The methodological principle that we follow in this study is that our ignorance of an author's motivations in no way authorizes the presumption that they are incoherent or faulty. We hold that until proven otherwise, Dante, as "a most prudent man" (*oculatissimo uomo*), could not have chosen his *incipit* lightly or superficially. On the contrary, precisely the fact that the comic title appears discordant with respect to what we know of the ideas of the poet and his age brings us to claim that it was carefully considered.

2. A precise study of the passages in which Dante speaks of comedy and tragedy demonstrates that this claim is textually founded.

We thus know that to Dante's eyes, the poetic project that gave birth to the great songs of the *Rime* seemed eminently tragic. In *De vulgari eloquentia*, he explicitly states that the tragic style is the highest of all styles and the only one appropriate to the ultimate objects of poetry: "well-being, love and virtue" (*salus, amor et virtus*).[6] A little later he defines the song [*canzone*], the supreme poetic genre, as

> a connected series of equal stanzas in the tragic style, without a refrain, and focused on a single theme, as I have shown when I wrote "Donne che avete intelletto d'amore." If I say "a connected series in the tragic style," it is because, were the style of the stanza comic, we would use the diminutive and call it a *canzonetta*.
>
> (iaequalium stantiarum sine responsorio tragica coniugatio, ut nos ostendimus cum dicimus "Donne che avete intelletto d'amore." Quod autem dicimus tragica coniugatio, est quia cum comice fiat hec coniugatio, cantilenam vocamus per diminutionem.)[7]

The poem's comic title therefore above all implies a rupture and a turn with respect to Dante's own past and poetic itinerary, a genuine "categorical revolution" that as such cannot have been decided upon without conscious and vital motivation. In a passage of the letter to Cangrande, Dante seems implicitly to affirm such an awareness of reasons for his choice. With a definition that formally repeats commonplaces of medieval lexicography,[8] Dante here introduces a discussion that cannot be found in any of his known sources. "Now comedy is a certain kind of poetical narration," he writes, "which differs from all others" (*Et est comoedia genus quoddam poëtice narrationis ab omnibus aliis differens*).[9] This privileged situation of the comic genre, which has no counterpart in either medieval or late ancient sources, presupposes an intention on the poet's part to alter semantically the term "comedy" in a sense that certainly goes beyond what modern criticism believes itself to have ascertained.

From this perspective, the fact that in the *Inferno* Dante explicitly defines the *Aeneid* as "high tragedy"[10] is every bit as significant as the fact that he titles his own "sacred poem" a comedy. This is so not only because he thus comes to oppose the Comedy to the work of the poet from whom he considers himself to draw "the beautiful style that has done me honor" (*lo bel stile che mi ha fatto onore*), but also because the definition of the *Aeneid* as a tragedy cannot be coherently reconciled with the criteria of the "peaceful beginning" and "foul end" indicated in the letter to Cangrande.

In an attempt to use one half of the problem as an explanation for the other half, it has been said that to Dante's eyes, the *Aeneid*, as a poetic narration in the high style, could only be a tragedy. In fact, according to a tradition that has its origin in Diomedes and that is still alive in Isidore of Seville,[11] the *Aeneid* figures in medieval treatises as an example not of tragedy as much as of that genre of poetic narration that was defined as *genus commune* on account of presenting the speech of both characters and the author. It is curious that, as has been occasionally noted, in medieval treatises the classification of the three styles—whose prototype is to be found in the *Rhetorica ad Herennium*[12]—does not necessarily coincide with that of the genres of poetic narration. Comedy and tragedy, which never entirely lost their dramatic connotation, were commonly listed alongside satire and mime in the *genus activam* or *dramaticon* (in which only characters speak, without the intervention of the author). The enumeration of styles, moreover, always involved a reference at least to the elegy,[13] and could never be exhausted in the comedy/tragedy opposition. The radicality with which the letter to Cangrande transforms this double classification into a tragedy/comedy antinomy—an antinomy that is at once stylistic and substantial, and with respect to which other poetic genres are quickly set aside[14]—is in itself a sufficient sign of a strong, conscious sense of these two terms.

From this perspective, the eclogue to Giovanni di Virgilio constitutes another piece of evidence. Here Dante alludes to his own poem with the expression *comica verba*.[15] The interpretation of this passage has been led astray by one of Boccaccio's glosses, which explains that "comica, id est vulgaria." The influence of this gloss has been so tenacious that even in the recent *Enciclopedia dantesca* one reads that, in the first eclogue, Dante resolutely identified "the comic in the vernacular." A text that could have shed light on Dante's choice of title thus became irrelevant, since the identification between comic style and the Italian language is clearly untenable.[16] An attentive reading of Giovanni's verse epistle demonstrates that the reproaches made to Dante by the Bolognese humanist have as their object not simply the use of the vernacular as opposed to Latin but rather the choice of comedy as opposed to tragedy. The expression with which Giovanni characterizes Dante's writing, *sermone forensi*, does not allude to the vernacular but rather corresponds to the *sermone pedestri* of the passage in Horace cited by Dante in his letter to Cangrande, as well as to the *cotidiano sermone* of medieval poetics.[17] *Sermone forensi*, in other words, refers to a choice of style and not language. This interpretation is confirmed by a further passage in the letter in which Giovanni, specifying his objections, encourages Dante to sing in "prophetic verse" the great facts of the history of his age, that is, the heroic and "public" material of tragedy instead of the "private" matters of comedy.

At the center of the debate with Giovanni di Virgilio, which belongs to the cultural circle from which the first modern tragedy, Mussato's *tragoedia Ecerinis*, was to be born, is not as much the Latin/vernacular opposition as the tragedy/comedy one. This testifies once again to the fact that for Dante, the comic title of his poem is neither contingent nor fragmentary, but rather constitutes the affirmation of a principle.

3. If this is true, then it is all the more dispiriting that the title of the Comedy is not compatible with the set of definitions given by Dante for the tragic/comic opposition, and that these definitions cannot, moreover, be reduced to a unitary system.

As has been noted, these definitions are articulated on two planes: a stylistic-formal one (the *modus loquendi*), and a material-substantial one (the *materia* or *sententia*). In *De vulgari eloquentia* (in which the stylistic aspect is prevalent and whose incompleteness is such that this work gives us no genuine thematic treatment of comedy), the tragic style is defined, according to the principles of the classical tripartition of styles, as the most elevated style (*superiorem stilum*), in harmony with the height of the material reserved for it (the three great *magnalia*: *salus, amore,* and *virtus*). In the letter to Cangrande, in which the material articulation is prevalent, the tragic/comic opposition is instead characterized on the plane of content and as an opposition of beginning and end: tragedy is marked by an "admirable" and "peaceful" beginning and a "foul" and "horrible" end; comedy by a "horrible" and "foul" beginning and a "prosperous" and "pleasant" end. On the stylistic plane, the tragic/comic opposition is presented as an opposition between what is, in one case, an elevated and sublime *modus loquendi* and, in the other, a "lowly" and "humble" *modus loquendi* (tempered, however, by a reference to Horace, who *licentiat liquando comicos ut tragicos loqui*).

Even a superficial examination of these categories demonstrates that according to the criteria of *De vulgari eloquentia*, the Comedy cannot justify its title without contradiction, though the *Aeneid* probably can be coherently defined as a tragedy. According to the criteria of the letter to Cangrande, by contrast, while the tragic justification of the *Aeneid* appears unfounded, the Comedy sufficiently justifies its title. The only thing that can in fact be affirmed with certainty is that in *De vulgari eloquentia*, Dante has in mind a tragic poetic project that is principally articulated on the stylistic plane, whereas the letter to Cangrande seeks to justify a comic choice defined in mainly material terms. No reasons for this change can, however, be identified. The only new element that appears in the letter to Cangrande is the peaceful beginning / harsh beginning, foul end / prosperous end opposition—that is, precisely the element that appears to our eyes as a mannered repetition of extremely superficial lexicographic stereotypes. This is so much the case that one of the oldest commentators and almost all modern scholars prefer to dwell on the stylistic-formal reasons, however deficient they may be, rather than accept the idea that Dante could have chosen the title of his own poem on the basis of such inconsequential considerations as the "foul" beginning of the *Inferno* (*a principio horribilis et fetida est, quia Infernus*) and the "pleasant" end of the *Paradiso* (*in fine prospera, desiderabilis et grata, quia Paradisus*).[18]

Yet when it appears that none of these reasons completely does away with contradiction, one may then ask whether the "material" arguments furnished by Dante in the letter to Cangrande are not in fact to be taken seriously, and whether their seeming superficiality even conceals an intention that criticism ought to make explicit. Perhaps the view that the Middle Ages had no experience of the comic and the tragic beyond a purely stylistic opposition, or beyond the crudely descriptive difference between a peaceful and a sad ending, derives from our reluctance to admit that the categories of the comic and the tragic—categories in which modernity, from Hegel to Benjamin, from Goethe to Kierkegaard, has projected its most profound ethical conflicts—may have their remote origin in medieval culture.

II. TRAGIC GUILT AND COMIC GUILT

1. The definition of the tragic/comic opposition given in the letter to Cangrande has until now been considered in isolation, without being placed in relation to its context. While this definition, or at least the part that interests us, concerns the work's "material" (*Nam si ad materiam respiciamus . . .*), the immediate context to which it must be brought back is the work's *subiectum*. A little later, Dante defines this "subject" in the following terms:

The subject, then, of the whole work, taken in the literal sense only, is the state of souls after death, pure and simple. For on and about that the argument of the whole work turns. If, however, the work be regarded from the allegorical point of view, the subject is man according as by his merits or demerits in the exercise of his free will he is deserving of reward or punishment by justice.

> (Est ergo subiectum totius operis, litteraliter tantum accepti, status animarum post mortem simpliciter sumptus. Nam de illo et circa illum totius operis versatur processus. Si vero accipiatur opus allegorice, subiectum est homo prout merendo et demerendo per arbitrii libertatem iustitie premiandi et puniendi obnoxius est.)[19]

The "prosperous" or "foul" ending, whether comic or tragic, therefore acquires its true meaning only when referred to its "subject": it thus concerns man's salvation or damnation or, in the allegorical sense, the subjection of man, in his own free will, to divine justice (*homo prout merendo et demerendo per arbitrii libertatem iustitie premiandi et puniendi obnoxius est*). Far from representing an insignificant and arbitrary choice on the basis of vacuous lexicographic stereotypes, the comic title instead implies the poet's position with respect to an essential question: the guilt or innocence of man before divine justice. That Dante's poem is a comedy and not a tragedy, that its beginning is "harsh" and "horrible" and its end "prosperous, desirable and pleasant" thus means the following: man, who is the work's *subiectum* in his subjection to divine justice, appears at the beginning as guilty (*obnoxius iustitie puniendi*) but at the end as innocent (*obnoxius iustitie premiandi*). Insofar as it is a "comedy," the poem is, in other words, an itinerary from guilt to innocence and not from innocence to guilt. And this is not only because in the book the description of the *Inferno* materially precedes that of the *Paradiso*, but also because the destiny of the individual named Dante, as well as the *homo viator* he represents, is comic and not tragic. In the letter to Cangrande, Dante thus joined the categories of the tragic and the comic to the theme of the innocence and guilt of the human creature, such that *tragedy appears as the guilt of the just and comedy as the justification of the guilty.*

This formulation, which appears so modern, is not something foreign to medieval culture that we have attempted to project on it here. The pertinence of the comic and the tragic to the theme of innocence and guilt is sanctioned by the text on which, implicitly or explicitly, every medieval conception of these two spheres is based: Aristotle's *Poetics.* Here the center of both the tragic and the comic experience is expressed with a word that is none other than the one by which the New Testament indicates sin: *hamartia.* It is curious that this terminological coincidence, by virtue of which tragedy and comedy could appear as the two poetic genres of antiquity at whose center lay *peccatum* (sin), has not been taken into account by scholars. Attention has been given mainly to late-ancient grammarians (such as Donatus and Diomedes) and lexicographers (such as Papia and Uguccione), although we know that the text of the *Poetics* was accessible in Latin both in partial form, through Herman the German's translation of Averroes's Middle Commentary, and in its entirety, through William of Moerbeke's translation.[20] If comic *peccatum* was characterized here as a *turpitudo non dolorosa et non corruptiva,*[21] the essence of the tragic affair was defined as a transformation of prosperity into bad luck, not through radical moral guilt (*propter malitiam et pestilentiam*) but through a *peccatum aliquod.* The presentation of a guilty person (*pestilens*) who went from bad luck to prosperity (*ex infortunio in eufortunium*) was, by contrast, treated as what was most antitragic (*intragodotatissimum*).[22]

In Averroes's paraphrase, the exclusion from tragedy of a subjectively guilty (*improbum*) character is understood in the sense that the essence of the tragic situation moves "from the imitation of virtue to the imitation of the misfortune into which the just have fallen" (*ex imitatione virtutem ad imitationem adversae fortunae, in quam probi lapsi sint*).[23] The paradox of Greek tragic *hamartia*— the conflict between a hero's subjective innocence and an objectively attributed guilt—is thus interpreted by positing at its center the misfortune of a "just person" (*probus*). With astounding sensibility, Averroes thus finds in the story of Abraham the tragic situation par excellence, anticipating Kierkegaard's own treatment of the matter: "and on account of this story, which tells the experience of Abraham, who was to kill his son, the greatest fear and terror is violently shown" (*et ob hoc illa historia, in qua narratur preceptum fuisse Abrae, ut iugularet filium suum, videtur esse maxime metum atque moerorem afferens*).[24] In an opposite sense, Averroes explicitly ascribes to comedy the representation of *vitium* (fault) from a perspective in which it does not appear as completely negative.[25]

2. It is in the context of this conception of tragic guilt and comic guilt that the title of the Comedy acquires its full weight and, at the same time, shows itself to be completely coherent. The "sacred poem" is a comedy because the experience that constitutes its center—the justification of the guilty and not the guilt of the just—is decisively antitragic. The *Aeneid*, by contrast, can only be a tragedy; its protagonist is a "just man" par excellence who, from the point of view of the *status animarum post mortem*, will nevertheless remain excluded from *iustitia premiandi* (Dante meets Aeneas in the first circle, alongside the souls that, even though guiltless, could not be saved). Aeneas, like Virgil, here represents the pagan world's condemnation to tragedy, just as Dante represents the "comic" possibility opened to man by Christ's passion.

Confirmation of the decisive importance of the peaceful or sad beginning of every human discourse on guilt can be found in a passage from *De vulgari eloquentia* whose essential connection with the problem of the Comedy's title has until now not been noted and which can, in fact, be seen as the secret mark with which the tragic poet of the *Rime* unconsciously announces the turn to the Comedy. Here Dante writes, with reference to Adam's first work in Paradise: "For if, since the disaster that befell the human race, the speech of every one of us has begun with 'woe!,' it is reasonable that he who existed before should have begun with a cry of joy" (*Nam sicut post prevaricationem humani generis quilibet exordium sue locutionis incipit ab "heu," rationabile est quod ante qui fuit inceperit a gaudio*).[26] If we keep in mind the later evolution of Dante's thought and place these words in relation to the "material" motivations in the letter to Cangrande, these words signify that *after the Fall, human language cannot be tragic; before the Fall, it cannot be comic.* At this point the critical problem of the Comedy's title changes, however, and must be reformulated in these terms: how could Dante, until a certain point, have held a tragic project to be possible? How, that is, could there be tragedy after the Fall and after Christ's passion? And, once again, how is it possible to join the impossibility of tragedy to the possibility of comedy, the *exordium ab heu* of every human discourse to the "prosperous ending" of comic discourse?

III. PERSON AND NATURE

1. Modern scholars have often repeated that a properly tragic conflict is not possible in the sphere of the Christian universe. Kurt von Fritz, the author of the efficient characterization of tragic guilt as the separation of a subjectively attributable guilt from an objectively grasped *hamartia*, considered the Christian conception of the world to be radically antitragic, excluding as it does the possibility of such a separation.[27]

While substantially correct, this statement is too peremptory. A conception of guilt that is certainly tragic is present in Christianity through the doctrine of original sin and the distinction between *natura* and *persona*, *natural* guilt and *personal* guilt, which the theologians elaborated and justified. For Adam's sin was not only *personal*; in him human *nature* itself sinned ("Your nature, when it sinned totally in its seed" [*Vostra natura, quando peccò tota / nel seme suo*]),[28] thus falling away from the natural justice that had been assigned to it by God.[29] As *natural* and not *personal* guilt, as guilt that falls to every man through his own origin (*peccatum quod quisque trahit cum natura in ipsa suo origine*),[30] original sin is a perfect equivalent of tragic *hamartia*. We can even say that precisely in its attempt to explain the paradox of guilt that is transmitted independently of individual responsibility through the distinction of natural sin and personal sin, Christian theology lay the foundations for the categories through which modern culture was to interpret tragic conflict. The Church Fathers conceive of original sin not as an actual and subjectively attributable sin but as an objective stain independent of will. This is so much the case, St. Thomas notes, that original sin is present even in children who lack free will.[31] The dispute between those who maintained that in Adam all humanity sinned *personaliter* and not only *naturaliter*, and the current orthodoxy, which holds fast to the natural character of original guilt, well shows the formation in Christian theology of this "natural" conception of guilt.

It is the confirmation of the natural character of original guilt that the Church Fathers found in the passage in Genesis (3:7) in which shame for one's own nudity appears as the first consequence of guilt. Thus if in St. Augustine's *De civitate Dei*, the loss of original justice and the birth of concupiscence, which withdraws the genital organs from the control of the will, are dramatically seen as the immediate penal consequences of the Fall, shame appears from the same perspective as the sign of the Fall's "natural" character:

> Human nature then is, without any doubt, ashamed about lust, and rightly ashamed. For in its disobedience, which subjected the sexual organs solely to its own impulses and snatched them from the will's authority, we see a proof of the retribution imposed on man for that first disobedience. And it was entirely fitting that this retribution should show itself in that part which effects the procreation of the very nature that was changed for the worse through that first great sin.[32]

> (Pudet igitur huius libidinis humanum sine ulla dubitatione naturam, et merito pudet. In ejus quippe inobedientia, quae genitalia corporis membra solis suis motibus subdidit, et potestati voluntatis eripuit, satis ostendetur quid sit hominis illi primae inobedientiae retributum: quod in ea maxime parte oportuit apparere, qua generatur ipsa natura, quae illo primo et magno in deterius est mutata peccato.)[33]

It is this dark "tragic" background that Christ's passion radically alters. Adequate to the guilt that man would never have been able to expiate, the passion carries out an inversion of the categories of *person* and *nature*, transforming natural guilt into personal expiation and an irreconcilable objective conflict into a personal matter. "This offence," the passage from St. Augustine cited above continues, "was committed when all mankind existed in one man, and it brought universal ruin on mankind; and no one can be rescued from the toils of that offence, which was punished by God's justice, unless the sin is expiated in each man singly by the grace of God."[34] Transforming the conflict between natural guilt and personal innocence into the division between *natural* innocence and *personal* guilt, Christ's death thus liberates man from tragedy and makes comedy possible.

Yet if man is no longer "the son of wrath,"[35] he nevertheless remains deprived of his original Edenic condition and of the coincidence between nature and person proper to natural justice. The salvation brought by Christ is not *natural* but *personal*:

> Salvation passes from Christ to man not via nature but via the work of good will, by which man adheres to Christ; and whatever follows from Christ is a personal good. Unlike the sin of our first parent, which was passed on by nature, such a personal good therefore cannot be transferred to others.
>
> (Effluxus salutis a Christo in homines non est per naturae propaginem, se per studium bonae voluntatis qua homo Christo adhaeret; et sic quod a Christo unusquisque consequitur est personale bonum; unde non derivatur ad posteros, sicut peccatum primi parentis, quod cum naturae propagine producitur.)[36]

The Fall continued to have penal effects, moreover, in concupiscence itself, which was the first consequence of guilt and which one exegetical tradition saw as the very vehicle for the transmission of sin. Perfect submission of the soul's sensible part to reason and will, which made possible blessed Edenic impassability and the nonlibidinal use of genital organs, remains closed off to man even after Christ's death. As St. Thomas writes, without noting the contradiction implicit in his letting a trace of Adamic *vetustas* survive at the heart of the redeemed universe:

> After baptism there remains both the necessity of death and concupiscence, which is materially contained in original sin. And thus the higher part of the soul participates in the miracle of Christ; but the souls of inferior men and the body itself remain in the original state that derives from Adam.

(Manet post baptismum et necessitas moriendi et concupiscentia quae est materiale in originali peccato. Et sic quantum ad superiorem partem animae participat novitatem Christi; sed quantum ad inferiores animae vires, et etiam ipsum corpus, remanet adhuc vetustas quae est ex Adam.)[37]

2. We may now understand why, to the eyes of the love poets and to the Dante of *De vulgari eloquentia*, love was a tragic experience. Insofar as it circumscribes the only sphere in which the "natural" character of original sin is conserved, love is in fact the only tragic experience possible in the medieval Christian world. It has been occasionally noted that the poets' introduction of love into the field of tragedy constitutes a novelty that cannot easily be explained. According to a tradition that is clearly expressed in a passage of Servius's commentary on the *Aeneid*[38] and that is still alive in Walther de Châtillon's twelfth-century classification of the *Veneris copula* among the *ridicula*, love was considered by late-ancient grammarians as the comic subject par excellence. It is precisely the conflict between the *natural* guilt of concupiscence and the personal innocence of the experience of love that makes possible the bold reversal by which love passes from the sphere of comedy to that of tragedy. It is in this conflict that we may locate the origin of the obstinately contradictory character of Provençal and Dolce Stil Novo love poetry that has so often divided modern critics, namely the appearance of this poetry as both the transcription of a base and sensual experience and the site of an exalted soteriological itinerary. The attempt to overcome this tragic conflict through the project of a complete repossession of original Edenic justice, that is, in the experience of a simultaneously *natural* and *personal* "perfection of love" (*fin'amors*), constitutes the powerful inheritance left by erotic poetry of the thirteenth century to modern Western culture.[39] From this perspective, Dante's "comic" choice acquires new weight. With respect to the "tragic" project of the love poets, the comic title of his poem constitutes a genuine "categorical revolution" that once again carries love from tragedy to comedy. In the theory of love set forth by Virgil in canto 28 of

the *Purgatorio*, the erotic experience ceases to be a "tragic" conflict between personal innocence and natural guilt and becomes a comic reconciliation of natural innocence and personal guilt. On the one hand he can thus affirm that "the natural is always without error" (*lo naturale è sempre senza errore*).[40] On the other hand he can deny the claim of "the people who aver that love is praiseworthy in itself" and—in opposition to Guido Cavalcanti's theory, according to which love implied the impossibility of correct judgment (*for di salute—giudicar mantene*)—can ground the personal character of amorous responsibility in an "innate . . . virtue, the faculty that counsels and that ought to hold the threshold of assent" (*innata . . . la virtù che consiglia, / e de l'assenso de' tener la soglia*).[41] Love thus withdraws from the dark tragic background of natural guilt to become a personal experience attributable to the individual's *arbitrium libertatis* and, as such, capable of being expiated *in singulis*.

3. This passage from natural, tragic guilt to personal, comic guilt is articulated through Dante's theory of shame, which is developed in canto 31 of the *Purgatorio*. Here Dante's expiation before his immersion in the waters of Lethe is accomplished through a process of "comic" humiliation that has at its center the experience of shame. If Dante had already felt shame before Beatrice and her severe apostrophe ("so great shame weighed on my brow" [*tanta vergogna mi gravò la fronte*]),[42] the purifying necessity of shame is confirmed immediately after Dante confesses his sin ("that you may now bear shame for your error" [*perché mo vergogna porta / del tuo errore*]).[43] The height of this "comic" humiliation comes when Beatrice turns to Dante, whom shame has made similar to a little boy ("as children stand ashamed and dumb" [*quali i fanciulli vergognando, muti*]),[44] with the following words: "lift up your beard" (*alza la barba*).[45] The meaning of this cruel joke can be clarified only if it is compared with the theory of shame developed by Dante in the *Convivio*, where one reads that shame is "good and praiseworthy" (*buona e laudabile*) "in women and in young people" (*ne le donne ne li giovani*), but "is not praiseworthy or suitable

in the elderly or in the virtuous" (*non è laudabile né sta bene ne li vecchi e ne li uomini studiosi*).[46] Above all, however, one must keep in mind the passage in which Oedipus, the tragic hero par excellence, is described as he who "put out his eyes, so that his shame would not appear without" (*si trasse li occhi, perché la vergogna d'entro non paresse di fuori*).[47]

The opposition could not be clearer between Dante, the "comic" character who purifies himself of personal guilt in showing the full extent of his shame, and Oedipus, the tragic hero who can neither confess his guilt nor accept shame insofar as he is *personally* innocent. What was, for the Church Fathers, the mark of the creature's natural guilt, which the tragic hero could not master, thus here becomes—through penitential humiliation—the instrument of reconciliation between man's personal guilt and creaturely innocence.[48] Immediately afterwards, the immersion in Lethe cancels even the memory of guilt.

Yet precisely because his comic choice above all signifies the renunciation of the tragic claim to innocence and the acceptance of the comic fracture between nature and person, Dante must at the same time abandon the love poets' attempt to return through perfect *joi* to an innocent, Edenic love. It is not by chance that Dante locates Arnaut Daniel and Guido Cavalcanti, as exemplary representatives of the erotico-poetic troubadour and Dolce Stil Novo project, precisely on the insuperable threshold of Eden. Matelda, the "lady in love" that Dante meets there, is indeed the symbol of the natural justice of the Edenic condition, as Charles Singleton's convincing arguments demonstrate.[49] But at the same time, she is the cipher of the impossible object of poetry and troubadour and Dolce Stil Novo eros; this is why Dante presents Matelda, genuine *senhal* that she is, in stylized and impersonal terms, and this is why the whole episode, as has been noted,[50] closely recalls the Provençal and Cavalcantian "pastorelle."

For Dante, original justice and the "sweet play" of the innocent, Edenic love in which nature and person once again coincide remain inaccessible to the human condition. In Western culture, the joy of love is—whether tragically or comically—divided.

IV. PERSON AND COMEDY

1. Dante's decision to call his poem a "comedy" therefore represents an important moment in the semantic history of two categories by which our culture has brought to consciousness one of its "secret thoughts." The antitragic turn that shows itself in this decision is not, however, a new and isolated event. In a certain sense, it represents the final act in a process to which late antiquity entrusted one of its deepest intentions. The division of Greek tragic drama, from whose sacrificial perspective tragedy and comedy still formed a whole, was already an accomplished fact in the fourth century B.C. This much is eloquently shown by Plato's own critique of tragedy. Yet it was through the Stoic critique, not the Platonic, that late antiquity transmitted its antitragic tendency to the Middle Ages. The Stoic critique of tragedy is developed through the metaphor of the actor, in which human life appears as a dramatic performance and men are presented as actors to whom a part (a *prosopon*, a mask) has been assigned. For the Stoics, what is tragic is not the mask in itself but the attitude, whether of attraction or repulsion, of the actor who identifies with it.[51] In a passage of the *Discourses* (which is most likely the immediate origin of the insistence with which late-ancient and medieval grammarians oppose comedy's *humiles personae* to tragedy's *reges, duces,* and *heroes*), Epictetus identifies the essence of the tragic situation—which is exemplified by Oedipus—in the confusion between actor and character:

> Remember that tragedies take place among rich people, kings, and tyrants. A poor man can take part in them only as member of the chorus. Kings begin with prosperity—"decorate the palace!"—but then, in the third or fourth act, they say, "Alas, Citero, why did you receive me?" Slave, where are the crowns and the diadems? Your bodyguards no longer obey you? When you meet one of these people, remember that you are meeting a tragic hero—not an actor but Oedipus himself.[52]

The wise man is instead the one who, accepting without discussion whatever "mask" has been assigned to him by fate, *represents* his part and thereby refuses to identify with it. From this perspective, the term *prosopon* changes meaning and, in contrast to "person" in the theatrical sense, begins to designate man's "moral personality," the power that furnishes criteria for action and that remains superior to all the possible acts it can produce.

On the one hand, "person" is thus the theatrical "mask"; on the other, it refers to the emerging notion of moral personality, a notion to which a properly juridical concept of the person is soon added. This juridical personality is already to be found in a passage of Theophilus's paraphrase of Justinian's *Institutions*, where we read that "insofar as they have no person [*aprosopoi ontes*], servants are characterized [*kharakterizontai*] by the master's person." It is on the basis of the double semantic heredity of the term "person," which thus signifies both "mask" and juridico-moral "personality," that the theologico-metaphysical notion of person is formed in the work of the Church Fathers.

This ambiguity is captured in its undivided, originary coherence in Boethius's *Contra Eutychen*. Boethius is still perfectly conscious of the theatrical meaning of the term *persona*, yet he seeks to convert it into a philosophical category by making it the equivalent of the Greek *hypostasis* in the sense of *naturae rationabilis individua substantia* (the individual substance of a rational nature). In a passage in which the importance of tragedy and comedy for the status of the person has its originary legitimacy, the difficulty of this crucial semantic change comes to light as a "lack of words":

> The word "person" seems to be borrowed from a different source, namely from the masks [*personae*] which in comedies and tragedies are used to represent the people concerned. . . . The Greeks, too, call these masks *prosopa* from the fact that they are placed over the face and conceal the countenance in front of the eyes: *para tou pros tous horas tithesthai* (from being put up against the face). But since, as we have said, it was by the masks that they put on that actors represented the individual people concerned in a tragedy or comedy—Hecuba or Medea or Simo or Chremes,—so also of all other men who could be clearly recognized by their appearance the Latins used the name *persona*, the Greeks *prosopa*. But the Greeks far more clearly called the in-

dividual subsistence of a rational nature by the name *hypostasis,* while we through want of appropriate words have kept the name handed down to us, calling that *persona* which they call *hypostasis.*[53]

Yet even for Boethius, the notion of *persona* always refers to a *natura* that is its *subiecta* and without which it cannot subsist.[54] The modern notion of person as inalienable subject of knowledge and morality does not exist in medieval culture, which still detects the originary theatrical sonority of the term and sees in it the set of individual properties that are added to human nature's *simplicitas.* For only in Adam (and in Christ) did nature and person coincide perfectly and could a personal sin contaminate all of human nature. After the Fall, person and nature remain—tragically or comically—divided and will coincide again only in the "last day" of the resurrection of the flesh. And it is precisely because nature and person do not coincide in the creature that the Church Fathers, taking up an ancient Stoic metaphor, can view human life as a *fabula,* a *comoedia* or *tragoedia mondana.* "For if our age were to conceive a prophetic spirit," we read in John of Salisbury's *Policraticus,* "it would be very well said that comedy is human life on earth, where everyone, having forgotten himself, expresses a foreign person" (*At si nostra tempora propheticus spiritus concepisset, dicetur egregie quia Comoedia est vita hominis super terram, ubi quisque sui oblitus, personam exprimit alienum*).

2. The comic title of Dante's poem must also be situated in this context. Here the antitragic distance between actor and "person" becomes a "comic" division between human nature (which is innocent) and person (which is guilty). The duality between Dante the historical individual and Dante the man in general, whose grammatical trace Singleton found in the opposition between "nostra via" and "mi ritrovai" at the beginning of the poem (and for which Gianfranco Contini sees an institutional sanction in the opposition of the literal and allegorical senses), actually has its foundation in the disjunction between natural innocence and personal responsibility that lies at the center of Dante's "comic" con-

ception. Far from emerging fully armed from the mind of Western man, the modern concept of person was in fact formed through a lengthy process to which the comedy/tragedy opposition was closely related. (From this point of view, it can even be said that the moral person-subject of modern culture is nothing but a development of the "tragic" attitude of the actor, who fully identifies with his own "mask." This is why in modern culture, while comedy—which refused identification with the *prosopon* all the more because it had at its center the figure of the servant, that is, the *aprosopos* par excellence—has conserved its mask, tragedy has instead been necessarily obliged to do away with it altogether.) The one who accomplishes the voyage of the Comedy is not a subject or an *I* in the modern sense of the word but, rather, simultaneously a *person* (the sinner called Dante) and human *nature* (according to Boethius's definition, the *specificato proprietas* that is *subiecta* to this person). And it is this unity-duality of nature and person that founds the specificity of the protagonist's status in the Comedy with respect to that of other medieval allegorical poems, from Alain de Lille's *De planctu naturae* to the *Roman de la rose*. For allegory, far from truly being a "personification," instead expresses precisely the impossibility of the person: it is the cipher through which a nature that has been petrified by guilt gives voice to its "lament" and seeks, without success, to overcome tragic guilt through personal destiny.[55] In this sense, the protagonist of the Comedy is the first "person" of modern literature. But that this person views himself as a comic character rather than as a tragic hero is certainly not a meaningless fact. That the name of Dante, the exemplary mark of a person, was "of necessity registered" (*registrato di necessità*)[56] on the threshold of Eden at the moment of the confession and expiation of personal guilt confirms the poet's renunciation of every claim to tragedy in the name of the creature's natural innocence.

Once again, it is this "comic" conception of guilt and person that makes it possible to explain Dante's attitude to law. In tragedy, law expresses the subjection of guilty human nature to destiny, a subjection that the hero cannot, in his moral innocence, overcome.

But in comedy, law becomes the instrument of personal salvation. The person is the "mask" that the creature assumes and then, in order to purify itself, abandons to the hands of the law. This is why in *De monarchia*, Dante can conceive of the redemption of humanity through Christ's passion in the cold terms of a legal trial that simply ends with the *punitio* inflicted by a *iudex ordinarius* (regular judge); and this is why the relation between guilt and expiation is always presented by the symbols and language of law. The meticulous edifice of the Comedy, in which modern ethical consciousness has such trouble finding itself, is nothing but the husk used by the creature's natural innocence to realize its personal expiation. But the "person," which is the site of this expiation, is neither an allegory nor the moral subject that modern ethics will make into the inalienable center of man. The "person" is instead a *prosopon*, a mask, the "foreign person" and the *risilis facies turpis aliqua et inversa sine dolore* of law and comedy.

It is this "comic" conception of the human creature, divided into innocent nature and guilty person, that Dante bequeathed to Italian culture. It is certainly possible to see in his choice a confirmation of the historical position on which scholars have so often insisted. Present in the culture of Dante's age were both the love poets' tragic project, which Dante once shared, and the seeds, interpreted in Italy by Mussato, that led, following the discovery of the tragic character of history, to the reaffirmation of tragedy in the modern era. These tendencies slowly came to prevail in modern culture, preparing the way for the century that, with a tragic claim, considered its own *Weltanschauung* to be conceivable through tragedy alone.[57] But in Italy these tendencies remained singularly inactive, and if Italian culture remained more faithful than any other to the antitragic inheritance of the late-ancient world, this is because, at the beginning of the fourteenth century, a Florentine poet decided to abandon the tragic claim to personal innocence in the name of the creature's natural innocence, leaving behind perfect Edenic love for the sake of comically divided human love, morality's inalienable person for law's "foreign person," and the kite's "lofty soaring" (*altissime rote*) "over things that are totally base" for the sparrow's "low flight" (*volare basso*).[58] The fierce mask left by a superficial hagiography to a tradition that almost immediately forgot the reasons for the Comedy's title is, in this sense, a comic mask: it is that of "our comedian" (*comicus noster*), as Filippo Villani defines him, lucidly, at the beginning of his biography.

§ 2 *Corn*: From Anatomy to Poetics

Fabulari paulisper lubet, sed ex re.
— Angelo Poliziano

I. HISTORIA

Two thirteenth-century, possibly Italian manuscripts contain the following *razo*:

> Raimon de Dufort and Lord Turc Malec were two knights from Quercy who composed the sirventes about the lady called Milday n'Aia, the one who said to the knight that she would not love him if he did not *corn* her in the arse.
>
> And here are written the sirventes.[1]

> (Raimons de Dufort e• N Turc Malec si foron du cavallier de Caersi que feiren los sirventes de la domna que ac nom ma domna n'Aia, aquella que dis al cavalier de Cornil qu'ella no l'amaria si el no la cornava el cul.
>
> Et aqui son escritz los sirventes.)

In the two sirventes that follow, however, as in Arnaut Daniel's tauter poem, which intervenes in the *gap*, the term designating the object of the "cornar" is not "cul" ("arse") but "corn."[2] Moreover, according to a precious intention that characterizes the impassable formalism of the poet whom Dante called "the better craftsman" (*il miglior fabbro*), *corn* is inscribed here at the center of a constellation of obscure and rare words that have furnished philologists with the occasion for somewhat uninspiring interpretative exercises. To summarize, let us open the dossier.

1. Ugo Cannello, 1883:

Cornar, meaning "to use sodomitically" in the sense at issue here, and thus *corn* for "bottom," are registered by neither the Lexicon nor the Glossary. But the metaphor of *corn* as "bottom" was common, as shown by Barbriccia in Dante's *Inferno*, XXI, 141, who made *del cul trombetta*. And there is the commentary to our passage in R. de Dufort's second sirventes, which is all too clear: "Se el no la cornava en cul."[3]

2. R. Lavaud, 1910:

Corn: Rayn. distinguishes *corn*, II, 485, "cor, clarion," from *corn*, II, 486, "horn, corner, angle, canal, pipe." Lévy combines all these senses in the same article, I, 369, and adds "behind, anus," following A. Dan. here and turc Malec (or rather Raimon de Dufort, according to Canello and me . . .). In this whole piece, the anus is compared to a trumpet, a clarion, or a horn." . . . In verse 6 *cornar* has its ordinary sense (cf. R., II, 486) of "to sound a horn or a trumpet."[4]

3. Gianluigi Toja, 1960:

Cornar: Canello's fanciful interpretation (p. 187), "to use sodomitically," was corrected by Lavaud, who proposed "to sound a horn or a trumpet," hence "to blow," a meaning deduced from the ordinary sense of *corn* (cf. SW., I, 368, which unites the words in *Lex.* II, 485: *cor, clarion* and in II, 486: *corne, coin, ancle, anal, tuyeau*, with the additional sense of anus, bottom).

Lavaud, taking away the drama of Canello's interpretation, has best understood the comic and realistic spirit of Arnaut's *pièce*.

On *corn* (= *cul*) there are no more doubts after the reading of IK and the allusions in 397, I, 15–16, 23–24 and 447, 1, II, 14, 42.

It seems that it is therefore a matter of an obscene "hole" exercise that has nothing to do with practices contrary to nature.[5]

4. Maurizio Perugi, 1978:

We are very far from resuscitating the improbable sodomical interpretation proposed by Canello; moreover, with all good will and imagination, we cannot succeed in understanding what this "hole exercise" consists in and how, in short, to represent it concretely (*honni soit qui mal y pense*). After close examination of the matter, and assuming that the men (and women) of the time were not substantially different from those of today with regard either to their physical structure, their sexual attitudes or the behavior inevitably connected to those attitudes, we believe that all the scholars from Canello onward were mistaken as to the part of the body at issue in the requested exercise. . . .

Before presenting the vouchers for our interpretation, let us consider more precisely the pertinent traits of *corn* as they can be found on the basis of extant sirventes. RDur speaks generically of *trauc sotiran* and of a mysterious *raboi* (III: 41: Contini reads "bottom" in conformity with his explanation of the entire tenson). ADan is richer in details: it situates the *corn* in the *efonil / enter l'eschin'e• l penchenil* (cf. vv. 41–42: the topographical detail surely corresponds to the vague *Cornatz m'ayssi sobre•l reon* [II 14]), and spends considerable time illustrating *que•l corns es fers e pelutz / que sta preonz dinz la palutz . . . e neül jorn no stai essutz* (cf. vv. 12–15). Now, without going any further, these details suffice to make us question the accepted interpretation: we agree on *fers*—but *pelutz*? And how to explain *essutz* with any likelihood?

Let us attempt to translate the complicated metaphor. *Corn* is assimilated to the tap of a barrel; we know that it is located in the "funnel" between the backbone and the pubic bone (ADan I, 41–42), that it is located in a marsh covered with hairs and that it is constantly humid (ADan I, 12–15). Raimon de Dufort says more generally that it is to be found *sobre•l reon* (III, 14), but above all he makes a distinction of great anatomical precision and vital exegetical importance with the words *Si•m mostrava'l corn e•l con* (III, 11). Therefore the *corn* is close to the *con* without being identical to it. On account of the metaphor continued in ADan and the connotations given to it, there can only be one answer: the *corn* is the clitoris.[6]

5. L. Lazzerini, 1981–83:

The current opinion, however, has found a fierce adversary in A.D.'s last editor, who, venturing in a few words into the dark recesses of feminine anatomy, presents in a little (para-) gynecological treatise the result of his laborious investigations, with the intention of demonstrating how and in what way *corn* was not what it had been thought to be, but rather something quite different (and more titillating). Let us say right away that this sensational performance, this kind of red-light "scoop" perpetrated at na Ena's expense, leaves one somewhat perplexed. . . . In reality, the arguments do not add up. Having first of all eliminated one *trauc* for the sake of the other, Perugi ends up doing away with both of them, since it is impossible to see which orifice could be attributed to the organ he so peremptorily identifies. . . . In addition to the doubts already mentioned, we are bothered by another critical point (A.D., vv. 24–25):

> que, si•l vengues d'amon lo rais,
> tot•ll' echaufera•l col e•l cais

For we do not see how a *rais* could threaten *amon* the knight of Cornhil, who is supposedly busy with a clitoris. It is, in fact, the case that all feminine *traucs* are unequivocally located below the erogenous zone Perugi identified as the *corn*.[7]

6. Mario Eusebi, 1984:

There would be no reason to repeat what a *corn* is if Perugi had not proposed an interpretation (II, pp. 3–10) that must be refuted. The substance of Perugi's argument is as follows. The *corn* cannot be the anus, because it is *pelutz* and is never *essutz* (p. 5); "[its] semantic field coincides almost perfectly with that of v. 47 *dosil*" (p. 8); because Raimon de Dufort, III, 11 says *Si•m mostrava'l corn e•l con*, "the *corn* is close to the *con* without being identical to it" (p. 9); hence "the *corn* is the clitoris" (p. 9). Now, (1) one can certainly not maintain that the anal orifice cannot be surrounded by hairs, nor can one claim that the rectum does not have a mucus of its own or that other secret viscous liquids (menstrual blood?) cannot wet the anus, which is located in the same *palut* as the sexual organs and in complete accord with the unpleasant effect that is sought. (2) The verse cited from Raimon de Dufort, III, 11, proves that the *corn* is not the *con*, just as what one reads immediately afterwards, 14, *Cornatz m'ayssi sobre•l reon*, locates the *corn* in the bottom. . . . Moreover, what is meant by this parodic inversion, as the exact opposite of the mouth? And *cornar* is naturally to be understood as "to bring the horn to one's mouth": *e no taing que mais sia drutz / cel que sa boc'al corn condutz* (vv. 17–18).[8]

II. ALLEGORY

The *Minnesänger* used the term *Korn* to signify "an unaccompanied verse that is at the center of a strophe, yet rhymes with the corresponding member of the following strophes."[9] The phenomenon is not unknown: it is the partially unrelated rhyme, which the Provençals call *rim'estrampa* or *dissolut* and which Dante, in *De vulgari eloquentia* (II, XIII, 5), terms *clavis* ("There are some, indeed, who do not always rhyme within a single stanza, but repeat them or rhyme them in later stanzas" [*Sunt etenim quidam qui non omnes quandoque desinentias carminum rithimantur in eadem stantia, sed easdem repetunt, sive rithimantur, in aliis*]).[10]

Matthias Lexer has a clear understanding of the function of *Korn* in strophic structure, writing that "the *Meistersinger* understood *Körner* to be the connection between two strophes through which a verse of the one rhymed with a verse of the other."[11] But in most German dictionaries, the term is listed among the senses of *Korn* as "grain," such that it becomes wholly inexplicable. Moreover, although the derivation of this metrical institution of the troubadour's technical poetics is certain,[12] the Old Occitan word *corn* is not listed in any lexicon as having this meaning, and therefore no documentation exists to support the idea that the Romance poets might have borrowed their term from the German.

At least this was the situation before Maria Careri, working on her edition of troubadour songbook H, twice came upon a gloss that, in order to mark a missing verse, noted the following: *aici manca us cor[n]s* (*cors* with an elongation mark on the "o," which Careri reads as *corns*).

"Cors," the editor writes,

> surely means "verse," metrical unit. It is unclear whether the word corresponds etymologically to *cursus* or to *cornus*. . . . It should be noted that in both this case and that marked in the Db2 gloss concerning Guiraut de Calanso's song (there in the form *I• cors I• faill*), the verse missing in H is a four-syllable one that rhymes with the immediately following verse (also a four-syllable verse in ArnDan, but a six-syllable

verse in GrCal). It is therefore possible that the term *cor[n]s* designates a special kind of verse.[13]

(It should also be noted, for the sake of accuracy, that in the Arnaut song at issue the two four-syllable verses, which are not technically *Körner*, metastrophically recall the two corresponding verses in the preceding *cobla*.)

The H scribe is therefore familiar with an unknown meaning of *corn*, one that refers not to feminine but rather to poetic anatomy and that, from now on, will have to be listed among the meanings registered in the relevant entry in Emil Levy's *Petit dictionnaire provençal-français*.[14] That this is not a matter of a forgettable *hapax* is immediately confirmed by H itself. In the first verse of the *tornada* of "L'aur'amara," H records not the usual *Faitz es l'acortz / qu'el cor remir* (which Lavaud translates as "this accord is concluded" and Perugi renders as "the accord has been stipulated"), but rather *Faits es lo cors quel cor remir*, that is, "the verse is made" (or, by synecdoche, "the poem is made"). Given the verse's location in the *tornada*, the sense of this version is far more satisfying (the proof is that Eusebi himself ends by interpreting *acort* as "rhyme": "the rhymes are over"). (As for the writing of *cor* or *cors* for *corn*, with the more or less intentional forgetting of the abbreviation mark, Eusebi compares it with other instances of the same kind in the manuscripts, such as, among others, precisely v. 47 of our sirventes.)[15]

It is unnecessary to underline the innovativeness of this lexical feature with respect to the whole corpus of courtly lyric poetry. The homophonic play of *cors* and *cor*, which is so important for the troubadours (as is the alliteration *cuer/cors* in the *trouvères*), turns out to be complicated by a third term that brings in a self-referential element, in which the anatomy of the body of love has a strict correlate in the poem's metrical structure. That the poem could be assimilated to a body in the context of courtly verse is, moreover, implicit both in the anatomical metaphors that proliferate in metrical terminology (the stanza's "feet," "face," and "tail"; the *capcaudada*'s "head-tail"; the "crippled" (*estrampa*) rhyme; *Laborintus*'s "stomach" verses) and in the equation between grammar and *nostra dona*, grammatical figures and erotic figures, that lies at the basis of *Las leys d'amors* and, therefore, of its obscene parody.[16] But this assimilation is explicit in Dante, when, in defining the *canzone*, he proceeds according to the soul/body paradigm; and it is also evident in the *Minnesänger*, who even use the word *Leiche* ("corpse") to name their supreme poetic institution.

We shall give only three examples, among the many possible passages found in Arnaut Daniel's work alone. In "Canso do-ill" it will be necessary to correct verse 54, so that it reads not *mos jois* but rather, as is found in manuscripts IKNSSg, *per que mos cors* (that is, *cor[n]s*) *capduelha*, "my verse reaches the summit" (this is indirectly confirmed by R, which has *mos chans*). Analogously, in XI, 25–26:

> Bona doctrina e suaus
> e cors clars, suptils e francx
> manda•m er al ferm condug.
>
> (A doctrine that is good and sweet
> And a *cors* radiant, gentle, and frank
> Have led me to the ledge of love.)[17]

The interpretation that suggests "precious, subtle, and frank verses" (H and R have *cars* instead of *clars*) displaces the poet's unlikely boastfulness onto his poetry, which makes altogether more sense.

Finally, imagine how the sestina's "marvelous contrivance" would be semantically complicated following the restitution of an archetype:

> Lo ferm voler qu'el corn intra
> no•m pot ges becs escoissendre ni ongla.
>
> (The firm will that enters into my *corn*
> With no beak or nail can ever be torn from me.)[18]

Here the firm will penetrates not into the lover's heart (whoever is familiar with the central function of the heart in medieval psychophysiology would expect the will to depart from it as from its source), but into the poem. Moreover, here we then find a serious appearance of the *becs/corn* approximation that is so characteristic of the sirventes. And if a little later, in verses 30 and 32, what would never leave the woman is not the heart but the poem, then Eusebi's excellent conjecture (according to which "the real subject of the entry into the *cambra* is song": *son . . . qu'apres dins cambra intra*)[19] would be finally confirmed.

As to *corn*'s etymological origin, there is no reason to do away with *cursus*; it suffices to relate it to one of *corn*'s meanings that is most well documented in the dictionaries: "tip," "extremity," "corner," "angle."[20] Just as "verse" draws its name from the point at which it is deployed (*versus*, which derives from *verto*, an origin with which the *Leys d'amors* is perfectly familiar: *girar* or *virar*),[21] so *corn* indicates the last part of a verse, which carries the unrelated rhyme.

III. TROPOLOGY

The legitimacy of a hypothesis must be verified above all through its function in specific contexts. If we return, therefore, to Arnaut's sirventes, the whole dispute surrounding Ayna's *corn* is displaced from its obscene literal sense to a question of poetic technique and from a problem of anatomical suitableness to a metrical matter. The "body of the woman = body of the poem" equation, which is not altogether unexpected but is still not a given, will find a counterpart in the equation of *corn* as bodily orifice and *corn* as point of rupture of the strophe's metrical structure. The poem's body, said by Dante to be "harmonized through the musical link" (*per legame musaico armonizzato*), is ruptured at one point, just as the integrity of the female body is broken in the *trauc sotiran*. But how is the reading of the text altered by this semantic displacement, which transforms a sexual prank into a poetic query? First of all, the otherwise improbable presence of the master of the *gradus constructionis excellentissimus* in an obscene tenson now turns out to have a precise reason. It happens that the problem of the unrelated rhyme in the strophe lies at the center of Daniel's technique, as Dante first notes with reference to the stanza that is "un-rhymed" (*sine rithmo*): "Arnaut Daniel used this kind of stanza very frequently, as in his *Se•m fos Amor de joi donar*" (*et huiusmodi stantiis usus est Arnaldus Danielis frequentissime, velut ibi, Se•m fos Amor de joi donar*).[22] Not only does Arnaut often make use of *corn*;[23] he also elevates the dissolved rhyme to the status of a new compositional canon in accordance with a metastrophic intention that profoundly marks his poetry.

Friedrich Diez noted this peculiar inclination of Daniel's *Lied*, which constitutes the logical premise for the invention of the sestina:

> Instead of joining the rhymes in the same strophe as usual, such that each strophe in itself constitutes a harmonic texture and a small *Lied*, he joins them only in the following strophe and leaves each rhyme to wait a whole strophe before finding its counterpart, thereby greatly weakening the effect of the rhyme. In Arnaut, this ordering of rhymes—of which there are also isolated examples in other troubadours—becomes the rule, and he allows himself only rare and significant exceptions to it. Hence the easy transition to the sestina.[24]

If, in short, one wanted to define Arnaut's style in one single trait that has its final apex in the sestina, one could say that *he is the poet who treats all verses as "corns" and who, by thus rupturing the closed unity of the strophe, transforms the unrelated rhyme into the principle of a higher relation.* The *Leys* states as much when, with limpid intuition, it finds in the *rim'estrampa* the compositional principle of Daniel's sestina: "And to understand what is meant by this near equality of syllables with a beautiful cadence, take, for example, the song by Arnaut Daniel that begins 'lo ferms volers que•l cor m'itra.' . . . We usually call such rhymes *estrampas*" (*E per que entendatz que vol dire quaysh engaltatz de sillabas am bela cazensa, podetz ayssi penre per ysshemple la canso que fo Arnaud Daniel can dish: lo ferms volers que•l cor m'itra. . . . Et aytals rimas apelam comunamen estrampas.*)[25]

From this perspective, the "body of the woman / body of the poem" equation, which constitutes the sirventes's secret theme, shows—at least at a first level—its full intelligibility. If the *corn* is a point of fracture in the unity of the strophe, and if the strophe's metrical structure is not to be irremediably shattered (with the consequent emission of *fum, glutz,* and *rais*), the laceration must take place with a particular precaution: the unrelated rhymes must be joined in a new metastrophic formal unity. Nothing less, that is, than what Arnaut explicitly asserts in *Doutz braitz*:

> e doncas ieu, qu'en la gensor entendi,
> dei far chanso sobre totz de tal obra
> que no• i aia mot fals ni rim'estrampa

> (Therefore I, who am aiming toward the fairest,
> Should make a song that will be of such fine work
> That there won't be a word that's false or a rhyme
> out of place [*rim'estrampa*].)[26]

(Here, of course, we must keep in mind, as Costanzo Di Girolamo has suggested, that Arnaut gives the name *rim'estrampa* to "what the *Leys d'amors* would later call *rims espars* or *brut*, which is to say completely unrelated rhymes.")[27] Only if the rhymes are thus metastrophically joined will it be possible to lay bare (and even kiss) the body of the woman-poem without danger. (On the basis of the parallelism with the *tornada* of "L'aur'amara," and in contiguity with the sirventes's *cornar•l corn,* in vv. 39–40 we thus read: *que•l sieu bels cors baisan, rizen descobra / e que•l remir contra•l lum de la lampa,* "to discover, kissing and laughing, her beautiful body, and to look upon it in the light of the lamp.")

According to the purest troubadour intention, the sirventes's obscene and playful theme is thus perfectly reunited with that grave "theorem of the predominance of the harmonic over the melodic" by which Contini, following Dante, grasped Arnaut's poetics.[28] The theorem is severe insofar as it places at the center of poetic composition a canon that is, in the extreme case, perceptible only in writing and that thereby prepared the way for the event that was soon to mark the history of the European lyric: the poetic text's definitive break with song (that is, with the element Dante called *melos*). For if it is true that in Occitan literature we can assume a correspondence between strophic division, which is marked by regular rhymes, and melodic division, it is just as certain that the *corn* or unrelated rhyme signals a point of rupture in this correspondence. And the new technique inaugurated by Arnaut, which elevates this fracture to the status of supreme compositional principle, will then signify such a radical metamorphosis of the body of the poem as to justify the tempestuous alchemical fermentation that seems to take place in the body of Ayna. At the point where the flat correspondence between metrical phrase and melodic phrase is broken, there arises a new and more complex correspondence in which the unrelated verse, binding itself to its counterpart in the following strophe, plays out a superior and, so to speak, silent score.

The change of the structure of song in the direction of *continuous ode* and antimelodic instrumentation does not, therefore, signify a musical choice. Instead it is the prelude to a radical crisis in the relation between the text and its oral performance. In this sense, Daniel's sestina is the first move in a secular game that has as its extreme checkmate Mallarmé's "Un coup de dés," and in which what is at stake is the emancipation of the poetic text not only from song but from all oral performance in general. "The page," Mallarmé will write, "taken as a unit, as is elsewhere the verse or the perfect line" (*La Page . . . mise pour unité comme l'est autre part le Vers ou ligne parfaite*).[29] In other words: poetry as something essentially graphic. This self-sufficiency of the written text was, after all, perfectly clear to Dante (despite the "song of love which used to quiet in me all my longings" [*amoroso canto / che mi solea quetar tutte le mie voglie*] of *Purgatorio* II, 107–8),[30] who has no doubt that "a piece of music as such is never given the name *cantio*" (*numquam modulatio dicitur cantio*) and that "even when we see such words written down on the page, in the absence of any performer, we call them *canzoni*" (*etiam talia verba in cartulis absque prolatione iacentia cantionem vocamus*).[31] Bonagiunta's reproach of Guinizelli, accusing him of "drawing song by the force of writing" (where "by the force of writing" must be read, as Guglielmo Gorni has suggested, as a syntagma),[32] must then be placed in the context

of this transition from a strongly oral compositional canon to one
in which writing has become completely autonomous. The game
played in the body of Ayna is this risky; it is this decisive.

IV. ANAGOGY

Only occasionally in modern works on metrical structures is rigorous description accompanied by an adequate comprehension of
the meaning of meter in the global economy of the poetic text.
Aside from hints in Hölderlin (the theory of caesura in the *An-
merkung* to the translation of Oedipus), Hegel (rhyme as compen-
sation for the domination of thematic meaning), Mallarmé (the
crise de vers that he bequeaths to twentieth-century poetry), and
Max Kommerell (the theological or, rather, atheological meaning
of *Freirhythmen*), a philosophy of meter is almost altogether lacking
in our age. Might it be possible to take a cue, in this sense, from
the special anatomy of Ayna's body? In any case, it is certain that a
poet's consciousness cannot be investigated without reference to his
technical choices.
    We have seen that as a point of rupture of the poetic body, *corn*
marks a disjunction between harmonic and melodic textures and
between orality and writing. But this metrical institution (like all
others) cannot be understood if it is not situated in the context of
a different formal opposition, namely, that between sound and
sense, metrical segmentation and syntactical segmentation. It is the
awareness of this opposition's eminent status that has led modern
scholars to identify in enjambment the only certain distinctive criterion for poetry as opposed to prose. (Poetry will then be defined
as that discourse in which it is possible to oppose a metrical limit—
which can, as such, also fall in the context of prose—to a syntactical limit; prose will be defined as the discourse in which this is not
possible.) Enjambment thus thematically marks the "rupture"[33] between metrical pause and syntactical pause that (as Georges Lote's
analyses of *pauza suspensiva* and *pauza plana* demonstrate)[34] also
characterizes caesura and rhyme, if to a minor degree. What is
rhyme, if not a disjunction between semiotic event (the repetition

of sounds) and semantic event, such that the mind searches for an analogy of sense in the very place where, disenchanted, it can find only a formal correspondence? (The question of the genesis of these institutions in modern poetry, which is almost insoluble *de facto*, can be easily answered *de iure* if one consistently considers it with reference to the harmony between sound and sense that defines the very site of poetry.)

Now, the authors of medieval treatises show themselves to be conscious of this opposition,[35] even if it is necessary to wait until Nicolò Tibino for a perspicuous definition of enjambment ("it often happens that the rhyme ends without the meaning of the sentence having been completed" [*multociens enim accidit quod, finita consonantia, adhuc sensus orationis non est finitus*]).[36] Moreover, on closer inspection it appears that Dante is perfectly aware of the absolutely fundamental significance of this opposition. In the very moment in which he defines the *canzone* with respect to its constitutive elements, he opposes *cantio* as unit of sense (*sententia*) to *stanza* as a purely metrical unit (*ars*):

> And here you must know that this word [*stanza*] was coined solely for the purpose of discussing poetic technique, so that the object in which the whole art of the *canzone* was enshrined should be called a stanza, that is, a capacious storehouse or receptacle for the art in its entirety. *For just as the canzone is the lap of its subject-matter, so the stanza enlaps its whole technique;* and the latter stanzas of the poem should never aspire to add some new technical device, but should only dress themselves in the same garb as the first.

> (Et circa hoc sciendum est quod hoc vocabulum [stantia] per solius artis respectum inventum est, videlicet ut in qua tota cantionis ars esset contenta, illud diceretur stantia, hoc est mansio capax sive receptaculum totuis artis. *Nam quemadmodum cantio est gremium totius sententiae, sic stantia totam artem ingremiat*; nec licet aliquid artis sequentibus adrogare, sed solam artem antecedentis induere.)[37]

Dante thus conceives of the structure of the *canzone* as founded on the relation between an essentially semantic, global unit and essentially metrical, partial units. It is remarkable that he expresses this contrast precisely through a bodily image: the feminine bosom, womb, or lap, with the implicit assimilation (suggested again a little later, *de ipso corpore*)[38] of the *canzone* to a body constituted by metrical organs (and the verb *ingremiare*, "to 'enlap' or to receive in the bosom, womb, or lap," can, like the corresponding verb *insinuare*, have an equivocal sense).

From this perspective, the unrelated verse (or *corn*) appears no longer merely as an instrument for the realization of metastrophic unity, but rather above all as the place of the border *per superexcellentiam* between metrical unity and semantic unity. It then becomes comprehensible why Dante, offering what appears to be an improbable suggestion, calls the unrelated verse *clavis* ("key," but also "nail," according to the double meaning of the term, which also corresponds to the originary unity of the thing; see the play between the two senses in *Paradiso*, XXXII, vv. 126–29: "the keys . . . with the nails" [*le chiavi . . . coi clavi*]). Insofar as it opens (or closes: *clavis quod claudat et aperiat*, Isidore, *Etymologiae*, XX, 13, 5) the closed formal womb of the stanza, the unrelated rhyme (the *corn*!) constitutes a threshold of passage between the metrical unity of *ars* and the higher semantic unity of the *sententia*. This is why, in Arnaut's skilled hands, it evolves so to speak naturally into a word-rhyme structuring the composition of the sestina: the word-rhyme—it must be stressed—is first of all a paradoxical point of undecidability between an eminently asemantic element (consonance) and an essentially semantic element (the word). In the point at which rhyme once attested to a disjunction between sense and sound, between understanding and the ear, there now stands a purely semantic, isolated unit, which frustrates the expectation of consonance, only then to reawaken and fulfill it at a point at which it is almost inaudible (if not entirely silent, "by the force of writing").

The body of poetry thus appears to be traversed by a double tension, a tension that has its apex in the *corn*: one tension that seeks at every opportunity to split sound from sense, and another that, inversely, aims to make sound and sense coincide; one that attempts to distinguish the two wombs with precision, and another that wants to render the two absolutely indistinct. The extreme case is *glossolalia,* in which sense and sound cannot be told apart: William IX's "babariol, babarial, babarian," or Nemrod's "Raphel may amèch zabì almì," both "before or beyond"[39] meaningful discourse.

V. SEU SENSUS MYSTICUS

The sentence in which Dante evokes the unrelated rhyme in *De vulgari eloquentia,* which we emphasized above, must be considered in this light. Here Dante almost underlines (somewhat disdainfully) the importance of the term, but without drawing on the troubadour tradition (he does not mention the instances of unrelated rhymes familiar to him in Arnaut, for example). Instead he refers to an otherwise unknown Gottus of Mantua (which should perhaps be read not as an improbable name but as "a German from Mantua," that is, as a reference not to a *Minnesänger* but to a Jew, as has been indicated to me by the subtlest scholar of thirteenth-century Italian Kabbalists, Moshe Idel, on the basis of the common equation of *Alemano* with Ashkenazik).

With his usual acumen, G. Gorni has noted the Dolce Stil Novo poets' characteristic use of unrelated rhymes, which Guinizelli, in the sonnet "Caro padre mio," seems explicitly to oppose, as a weak tie, to rhyme as the "canonic knot" of the poetic composition.[40] (It is significant that Dante's negative archetype, Guittone, takes the greatest care to avoid unrelated rhymes.)

Keeping in mind the dignity assigned to the key-verse (or nail-verse) in the economy of courtly poetics may allow for a less naive (or at least less contradictory) reading of Dante's summary definition of the Dolce Stil Novo in canto XXIV of *Purgatorio.* The trivial reading of this definition romantically distorts Dante's theme by interpreting it as suggesting a link between sense and sound, text and dictation, that is closer than the one in Guittone (this is the mythological "sincerity of expression" scorned by Contini). Such a reading is proven false by, among other texts, Dante's theory of poetic enunciation, which he develops in chapters 3 and 4 of Book III of the *Convivio* and which must now be returned to its proper programmatic status. Here Dante defines the poetic event not by a convergence but rather by a divergence between intellect and language. This divergence gives rise to a double "ineffableness" (*ineffabilitade*), in which the intellect cannot grasp ("end") what language says and in which language does not "completely follow" what the intellect comprehends:

> For in speaking of her my thoughts many times desired to conclude things about her which I could not understand, and I was so bewildered that outwardly I seemed almost beside myself. . . . This is one ineffable aspect of what I have taken as my theme; and, subsequently, I speak of the other. . . . I say that my thoughts—which are the words of Love—"have such sweet sounds" that my soul, that is, my affection, burns to be able to tell of it with my tongue; and because I am not able . . . this is the other ineffable aspect: that is, that the tongue cannot completely follow what the intellect perceives. . . . I say then that my insufficiency derives from a twofold source, just as the grandeur of the lady is transcendent in a twofold manner, in the way that has been mentioned. For because of the poverty of my intellect it is necessary to leave aside much that is true about her and much that shines, as it were, into my mind, which like a transparent body receives it without arresting it; and this I say in the following clause: *And surely I must leave aside.* Then when I say *And of what it understands* I assert that my inability extends not only to what my intellect does not grasp but even to what I do not understand, because my tongue lacks the eloquence to be able to express what is spoken of her in my thought.[41]

It is well to investigate this extremely dense passage, in which Dante proposes nothing less than a new and, even today, largely unconsidered conception of the poetic act. Take the text in St. Thomas that constitutes Dante's immediate model:

> Whenever speech is the cause of the intellect, as in those things learned by instruction, what the intellect grasps is not equal to the power of speech; and the intellect can then hear, but not understand the things spoken. . . . But whenever the intellect is the cause of speech, as in those things known by invention, then the intellect exceeds speech, and many things are understood that cannot be spoken.

> (In quibusdam locutio causat intellectum, sicut in his quae per disciplina discuntur: unde contingit quod intellectus addiscens non per-

tingit ad virtutem locutionis; et tunc potest loqui ea quae audit, sed non intelligit. . . . Quandoque autem intellectus est causa locutionis, sicut in his quae per inventionem sciuntur; inde in his intellectus locutionem excedit, et multa intelligantur quae proferri non valent.) (I *Sent.*, d. 37)

Here the philosopher clearly locates the process of learning in a double disjunction between the intellect and speech in which language exceeds the intellect (speaking without understanding) and the intellect transcends language (understanding without speaking). While Thomas, however, limits himself to opposing two distinct and in every sense separate modes of learning (learning by discipline and learning by invention), Dante's genius consists in his having transformed the two into a double but nevertheless synchronous movement traversing the poetic act, in which invention is inverted into discipline (into listening) and discipline is inverted into invention, so to speak by virtue of its own insufficiency. What follows is neither an anachronistic poetics of the intimate conjunction of sound and sense, speech and understanding, nor a flat and equally abstract rhetoric of the ineffable. Rather, here poetry is defined by a constitutive disjunction between the intellect and language in which, while language speaks without comprehending ("almost moved by itself" [*quasi da sè stessa mossa*]), the intellect comprehends without being able to speak.

This is why Dante can present this constitutive insufficiency ("the weakness of the intellect and the inadequacy of our power of speech" [*la debilitade de lo' ntelletto e la cortezza del nostro parlare*]) as "a fault for which I should not be blamed" (*una colpa de la quale non deggio essere colpato*), for which he has reason "simultaneously" to accuse and exonerate himself. These two synchronous and inverse processes in the act of speaking (and listening)—that of language's movement toward comprehension and of comprehension's movement toward language—communicate with each other in their limitation, such that (as Dante will go on to say) their imperfection actually coincides with their perfection (*Convivio*, III, 15, 9).

If this is the structure of the poetic dictation, the terzinas of *Purgatorio*, XXIV, 49–63, will have to be reread. First of all, the double

scansion *spira/noto* and *detta / vo significando* (as in the *I'/un* dupli-
cation) corresponds to the *Convivio*'s double excess and double ineffability, which—once definitely taken as a felicitous poetic principle—delimits the space in which, according to Dante's central
intention, invention is transformed into listening (and transcription) and listening into invention. The "close" (*strette*) movement
of the pen "following after" (*di retro*) the dictator cannot therefore
signify a simple obedience. Rather, insofar as the pen follows the
dictation through its very insufficiency, "close" must be understood
in the sense of "hampered, with difficulty," as when it is referred
to speech in the Comedy (see, above all, *Purgatorio*, XIV, 126: "so
has our discourse wrung my heart" [*sì m' ha nostra ragion la lingua
stretta*]).[42] But the *nodo / ch'i'odo* rhyme, which often appears in the
Comedy in such significant contexts (*Paradiso*, VII, 53–55; *Purgatorio*, XVI, 22–24), also cannot be accidental. It is even possible to
find in this rhyme a barely disguised evocation of the very "nail"
(or "key") that we have seen to mark the connection-disjunction
(almost the unrelated relation) of sound and sense in *De vulgari
eloquentia* (while the "knot" [*nodo*] will then inversely mark the ar-
rogant attempt to make sound and sense coincide, as in Marcabru,
"la razon e•l vers lassar e faire"). And does not Guinizelli reveal as
much in the clearest fashion when, a little later, he cites Bonagiunta's words and says: "You leave, by that which I hear, traces so
deep and clear in me that Lethe cannot take them away or make
them dim" (*Tu lasci tal vestigio / per quel ch'i' odo, in me, e tanto
chiaro / che Leté nol può trarre né far bigio*)?[43] The Bonagiunta
episode thus dramatizes in almost Cavalcantian terms the same felicitous disjunction that the *Convivio* articulates in the form of
doctrine and that can be overcome only by the divine mind, in
which the intellect and its object coincide. For every human claim
to transcend this disjunction loses sight of the distance that sepa-
rates the two "styles" (the writing of language, which exceeds the
intellect, and that of comprehension, which exceeds language):
"and he who sets himself to seek further can see no other difference
between the one style and the other" (*'e qual più a gradir oltre si
mette / non vede più da l'uno a l'altro stilo'*).[44]

And is this not precisely what happens in every genuine poetic enunciation, in which language's movement toward sense is as if traversed by another discourse, one moving from comprehension to sound, without either of the two ever reaching its destination, the one to rest in prose and the other in pure sound? Instead, in a decisive exchange, it is as if, having met each other, each of the two movements then followed the other's tracks, such that language found itself led back in the end to language, and comprehension to comprehension. This inverted chiasm—this and nothing else—is what we call poetry. This chiasm is, beyond every vagueness, poetry's crossing with thought, the thinking essence of poetry and the poeticizing essence of thought. And in this crossing (in which, as at every crossroads, catastrophe is always possible) it is the "nail" (or "key") that constitutes the mechanism of exchange, just as it is the *corn* that marks the trace of this exchange in the delirious body of Ayna.

VI. EPILOGUE

But who is Ayna, this being made of both words and sound, whom we have explored in searching after the limit of the anatomy of love? Sharp, lively, and almost chaste in her shamelessness, she certainly appears as an inverted figure of the troubadour's *domna genser que no say dir*, and of the "Lady Intelligence" that the love poets present as both the origin and the destiny of their song. As such, she calls to mind the "stammering woman" (*femmina balba*) of *Purgatorio*, XIX, 7–15, the babbling siren whose appearance gives rise to just as indecent an exhibition and in whom critics have rightly seen a figure of "non-song."[45] Here, however, even the inversion is complicated and, so to speak, in turn inverted.

We believe that we have identified the archetype in a passage of Eriugena's glosses on Martianus Capella, a text that was certainly not unknown to courtly culture. Here we read, with reference to one of the Muses' names:

ANIA, intellect. For NIA is intellect, hence the expression NOYS. "A" signifies many things for the Greeks. Sometimes it denotes a negation;

sometimes it denotes an addition, as in this name ANIA: here "A" increases its sense.

(ANIA, intelligentia. NIA enim intelligentia, ab eo quod est NOYS dicitur. A apud Grecos multa significat. Per vices enim negat, per vices implet, sicut in hoc nomine ANIA: ibi enim auget sensum.)[46]

Ayna is exactly the inverse of Ania. But just as for Eriugena, "A" is not privative but intensive, so the inversion of Ayna into comprehension is not simply negative. Rather, it is carried to the point (which the act of *cornar* parodically expresses) at which comprehension is darkened in speech and speech is silenced in comprehension. Insofar as it bears the *corn*'s coat of arms, her oneiric body is the place offered by the poet to unrelated relation and, almost, to the reciprocal catastrophe of sound and sense that defines poetic experience. That she appears in Raimbaut d'Aurenga's "No say que s'es," that is, in a poetic composition whose extreme novelty consists in its keeping itself in both poetry and prose, will certainly not seem incongruous at this point. The site of a fulfillment and an impossibility, of a perfection possible through an imperfection alone, Ayna is, perhaps more than any other feminine *senhal,* the final cipher of the troubadour project, the *flor enversa* revealed on the very threshold of the terrestrial paradise in which only Matelda (once again an inverted name: *ad letam*) performs her innocent dance. And only after having consigned this dream to its anagraphic identity can we take leave of it.

§ 3 The Dream of Language

To Giovanni Pozzi and Carlo Dionisotti,
Who Cleared the Way for Every Reading of Polifilo

I

The observations that follow seek to locate a famous yet little-read work in the site that is proper to a reading and, in so doing, to return it to a dimension in which its material content and its truth content (or, we could also say, taking up the medieval theory of the many senses of Scripture, its literal sense and its allegorico-moral sense) coincide. If it is true that every reading of a work must necessarily reckon with the growing distance between different levels of meaning that is caused by time, it is also true that a genuine reading takes places only at the point at which the work's living unity, first present in the original draft, is once again recomposed.

In the case of the anonymous incunabulum printed in Venice in 1499 that is our subject here, *Hypnerotomachia Poliphili*,[1] any attempt to assume this task must confront a number of particular problems. First there are the difficulties posed by a work that is over 500 years old and that comes from a milieu—fifteenth-century humanism—that has never succeeded in gaining a modern public. More decisive is the fact that the incunabulum, closed in its perfect Aldine jacket, seems to be composed of elements so divergent as to make it appear from the beginning a dead specimen without precedent or descendants, a kind of emblem in which—to use the terminology of those allegorical treatises that often took their inspiration from it—the ingenious will of the author irrevocably separated and silenced "soul" and "body." Even the beautiful illustrations that contributed to the book's good fortune add to this hieroglyphic and generally tomblike impression. And yet even if it certainly registered the problem of death, *Hypnerotomachia* was not a simple, pedantic exercise substantially foreign to the living part of the Italian literary tradition. Rather, it expressed in an exemplary fashion the crisis of one of the deepest intentions of the Italian tradition. Perhaps the philological obsession and the exacerbated love of language that characterize fifteenth-century humanism and the bilingualism that is at issue in it (and which is present in Italian literature, in different forms, from one end to the other) conceal a problem that is more essential than we are accustomed to think. The modest motto that Poliziano attributed to *Lamia*'s prologue (*grammaticus, non philosophus*), and that a text close to those we are concerned with here formulates as the fear of appearing as a "bad philosopher" rather than a commentator (*ne philosophaster magis videatur quam commentator*), therefore suggests that the more a work seems to concentrate on philological and linguistic problems, the denser its truth content may be. It is perhaps precisely here that the critic must not fear the risk of thought, and that the commentator, in turn, must not shy away from appearing as a "bad philosopher."

II

The necessary introduction to every reading of Polifilo is constituted by analysis of its language. The effect of estrangement that its language produces so disorients the reader that he literally does not know what language he is reading, whether it is Latin, the vernacular, or a third idiom—perhaps the one that a sixteenth-century parody early on defines precisely as the *lingua poliphylesca*. It is not simply a matter of an effect due to the text's temporal distance from us. The awareness of this effect was so central to the author and the first readers of the book that we find it clearly stated in the margins of the book itself. In the Latin letter of Leonardo Crasso that opens the text, we read: "The one wonderful thing about it is that while it speaks in the language of our country, considerable work is required to ascertain whether it is in Greek and Latin or Tuscan and the vernacular" (*Res una in eo mirando est, quod, cum nostrati lingua loquatur, non minus ad eum cognoscendum opus sit graeca et romana quam tusca et vernacula*) (I, IX). What is perfectly captured here is what still disturbs the modern reader, even if it is not at all clear whether we are to understand "the language of our country" as the Latin in which Leonardo writes or the text's own vernacular.

The anonymous elegy to the reader that follows a little later confirms these ideas by speaking of a "novel language and novel speech" (*nova lingua novusque sermo*) (I, X). Even more explicitly, Matteo Visconti's poem, added to the copy of the text in the Berlin Staatsbibliotek, refers to an "invention of a new and almost divine speech" (*novum propemodumque divinum eloquium nactus*) (II, 36).

Modern scholars have analyzed Polifilo's language, albeit not exhaustively. The results to which they were led confirm what appears to be the case at first glance: the book's language is a monstrous *unicum* in which a Latin lexicon is vigorously grafted onto the vernacular language at the work's foundation. In the words of one scholar who took exemplary care in studying *Hypnerotomachia*, the text is "an attempt to resolve the humanistic debate over Latin and vernacular with a practical formula, preserving the phonological and morphological reality of one and the lexical nobility of the other."[2] It is not simply a matter of the intrusion of purely Latin (and at times Greek) words into the vernacular lexicon, according to a process of growth that certainly characterized the history of the vernacular in the fifteenth century. Rather, here innumerable new linguistic formations are made through the separate transposition of Latin roots and suffixes, which lend life to words that are grammatically possible but that in reality never existed, and whose life remains mainly confined to their single appearance in Polifilo's dream.

Yet the sense of the operation performed on the lexical element is not fully understood if it is not placed in relation to the particular grammatical and syntactical structure of the work's prose. If *Hypnerotomachia*'s prose, on the one hand, captures the long and complex syntax of Boccaccio's style, on the other it complicates and burdens that syntax with a series of delays and anomalies[3] that ultimately leave the lexical element clearly stranded, appearing all the more alien in the discursive context of the text's propositions.

An intent of this kind—and, moreover, one which is consciously carried out—has been noted in Mallarmé,[4] where the infinite syntactical complication of the poet's writing makes words stand out in their isolation while their semantic values are suspended in what Mallarmé called an *isolement de la parole*. Thus, Mallarmé writes, words, held back in "vibratile suspension," are perceived by the mind independent of their contextual syntactical connection, in a kind of pure self-referential mirroring:

> Words rise up unaided and in ecstasy; many a facet reveals its infinite rarity and is precious to our mind. For our mind is the center of this hesitancy and oscillation; it sees the words not in their usual order, but in projection (like the walls of a cave), so long as that mobility which is their principle lives on, that part of speech which is not spoken.[5]

> (Les mots, d'eux mêmes, s'exaltent à mainte facette reconnue la plus rare ou valant pour l'esprit, centre de suspens vibratoire; qui les perçoit indépendamment de la suite ordinaire, projetés, en parois de grotte, tant que dure leur mobilité ou principe, étant ce qui ne se dit pas du discours.)[6]

It is this play between the lexical and the syntactico-grammatical elements that, in Polifilo, produces the effect of immobility and almost pictorial rigidity that has been noted by the critics. And it is this very play that the work's illustrations, like mirrors, seem to multiply. We find ourselves before a language in which the lexical element appears to prevail over the syntactico-grammatical element, before an agrammatical language, as has been said. More precisely, it is a matter not of an agrammatical discourse but rather of a language in which the resistance of names and words is not immediately dissolved and rendered transparent by the comprehension of the global meaning; hence the lexical element remains isolated and suspended for a few seconds, as dead material, before being articulated and dissolved in the fluid discourse of sense.

Polifilo's language is therefore a discourse in the vernacular that carries within it the lexical skeleton of Latin names, leaving it for an instant to appear in the background of its own coat of arms. We can then say that we find ourselves faced with a text in which one language—Latin—is reflected in another—the vernacular—in reciprocal deformation. *What the vernacular contains in itself without expressing—what remains unsaid in discourse—is thus in this case another language, Latin.*

Hence the impression of *festina lente*, of an excited delay and breathless lingering in these pages, whose rhythm is as if slowed down from within. Hence also that "insoluble uncertainly between humanistic and fourteenth-century elements" by which Dionisotti so perfectly summarizes Polifilo's character. Hence, finally, the sepulchral and dreamy rigidity of a prose in which discourse counts not for what it says but for what seems to remain unsaid and, nevertheless, to be present in it: exactly as in a dream, or in an acrostic, just as the names of both the author and the beloved are secretly hidden *in latine* in the initials of every chapter: *Poliam frater Franciscus Columna peramavit.*

III

These observations on language must now guide us in the reading of *Hypnerotomachia*, if a work's material content cannot be separated from its truth content and the language in which a work is written cannot be irrelevant to the work's material content. The book is the story of a dream, and at the center of this dream lies the figure of a woman, Polia. The male protagonist's love for Polia is so unusual and so obsessive that he has no reality other than that concealed in the name Polifilo: Polia's lover. The whole matter can be described as a "voyage into the amorous flames of Polia" (I, 113). Who is Polia? Answers to this question have traditionally been directed toward the historical, anagraphic deciphering of the real woman who would have been hidden under this name (for example, the niece of Teodoro de' Lelli, bishop of Trento), or else toward the deciphering of the name's allegorical meaning (for example, antiquity). It is obvious that for all their preciousness, such investigations can add little to the comprehension of the work as long as they do not confront what constitutes *Hypnerotomachia*'s textual specificity.

What do we know about Polia? Above all what the name itself says. Though it may seem surprising, Polia (from the Greek *polios, polia*) means simply "the gray woman, the old woman," and Polifilo simply means "he who loves the old woman." A reading of the marginal additions to the text (some of which were presumably written out by the author himself) makes it possible to add significant determinations to this given, which in itself is not transparent. First of all, the book's dedication informs us that Polia, the book's sole owner and addressee, is also the one who "painted" (*depinto*) and "made" (*fabricato*) the book: "which book," we read, "you, being its sole owner, have diligently painted in the amorous heart with a golden arrow, and sealed and made with your angelic effigy" (*tu industriosamente nell'amoroso core cum dorate sagitte in quello depincto et cum la tua angelica effigie insignito et fabricato hai, che singularmente padrona il possede*) (I, 2). Polifilo merely translated the book from its "first style" (*principiato stile*) into its present form, such that Polia, "great worker of the mind" (*optima operatrice e clavigera della mente*), would not receive blame for its faults.

Andrea Bresciano's poem informs us, moreover, that Polia, whose name identified her as "the old woman," is in fact already dead. Bresciano tells us that she lives again, dead, only thanks to Polifilo's dream, which makes her lie awake on the lips of the learned:

> O quam de cunctis felix mortalibus una es,
> Polia, quae vivis morta, sed melius:
> Te, dum Poliphilus somno iacet obtrutus alto,
> Pervigilare facit docta per ora virum.
> (I, XV)

> (O Polia, who among all mortals is the only
> happy one, you live in death; but you live better. While Polifilo lies destroyed in his deep
> sleep, he makes you stay awake on the lips of
> the learned.)

In the two epitaphs with which the book ends, Polia's death (or, rather, her dead life) is confirmed even more explicitly: Polia "lives buried" (*Felix Polia, quae sepulta vivis* [I, 460]), and Polifilo awakens her from her sleep. And in the words that Polia herself utters from the grave, in which the book itself seems to appear as her mausoleum, Polia is nothing but a desiccated flower that will never live again and that Polifilo has tried in vain to reanimate: "Alas, Polifilo, desist—a flower so desiccated will never live again" (*Heu Poliphile / desine / flos sic exsiccatus / nunquam reviviscit* [ibid.]).

Polia, the object of the author's amorous quest, is therefore not only an old woman; she is a dead woman, a woman brought to life by the dream alone, a woman who has in the book both her work and her mausoleum. Why? What does Polia's death mean? All these givens, which at first glance are impenetrable, become perfectly clear if we refer them not to a presumed referential reality but—once they are situated in the living unity of reading—to what we have observed regarding Polifilo's language and its self-referential nature. Polia, we may now advance as our first hypothesis, is old (language), dead (language), that is, the same Latin that Polifilo's novel text, in its archaic lexical rigidity, reflects into vernacular discourse in a reciprocal and dreamy mirroring. And Polifilo—he who loves Polia—is a figure for love of Latin: an impossible or dreamy love, since it is the love of a dead language, a love that seeks to reanimate the desiccated flower by transplanting it into the living members of the vernacular. Into Polifilo's *own* members, that is, if Polifilo—he who loves Latin—is therefore himself the figure of the mother tongue separated from Latin, whose love, according to the words of the first letter to Polia, necessarily means being fully alive in the other and completely dead in oneself (I, 439). For dead Latin words, suspended in their isolation, reappear and come alive again at the end, if it is true that, in the last analysis, we understand Polifilo's text, albeit with difficulty. The reflection of one language into another does not remain inert; it is not only the mirroring of two separate realities. Instead, here, as in every human discourse, something lives and something dies. The language of *Hypnerotomachia* therefore contains an implicit but articulated reflection on language, a theory of the relations between the vernacular and Latin that must be brought to light. The acrostic reveals not only the author's name but also the essential and irreducible bilingualism whose circularity is already inscribed in the passage from the Latin title to the vernacular text and, again, to the final Latin epitaph.

While leading the text to the site of a possible reading, this provisional hypothesis concerning Polia's identity also returns it to the historical context in which it was born: fifteenth-century humanism and the fracture of its rhetoric into Latin and the vernacular. For, according to a paradox that is only apparent, it was precisely the humanists who, in their passionate vindication of Latin, first formulated the idea of a life, senescence, and rebirth—but, by that very token, also of a *death*—of language. It was precisely the humanists who, in other words, first conceived of the object of their living love as a dead and reborn language.

IV

H. W. Klein has already reconstructed the birth of the concept of dead language in humanism.[7] Here it suffices to recall that it was Lorenzo de' Medici who, in the "Commento sopra alcuni de' suoi sonetti" ("Comment on Some of His Sonnets"), which antedates the printing of *Hypnerotomachia* by about fifteen years, first attempted to compare the development of a language to that of a living organism, establishing a parallelism between the ages of man and those of language. "The childhood of this language until now can be said to be very great, since it is becoming more and more elegant and pleasant. And it might attain even greater perfection in its youth and adulthood." Only a little later, after speaking of the death of the woman to whom the sonnets are dedicated, Lorenzo states the principle (which was later, in a famous dialogue by Varchi, to be textually transferred to language) according to which "it is doctrine among good philosophers that the corruption of one thing is the creation of another."

Many years before, in a text that constitutes the first history of Latin literature, Sicco Polenton's *Scriptorum illustrium latinae lin-*

guae libri XVIII, the equation of language with a living organism was expressed in the metaphor not of birth and rebirth but of a sleep and reawakening of language. Referring to the renewal of Italian culture in Dante's age, Sicco describes in charming detail the reawakening of the Latin Muses after a slumber of over a thousand years: "at that moment, like those who are still asleep, they began to move their limbs, rub their eyes, and stretch out their arms" (*hoc vero tempore, ut somnolenti solent, membra movere, oculos tegere, brachia extendere coeperunt*).[8] Yet in the preface to the first book of the *Elegantiae*, at the moment he states his passionate program for the restoration of the Latin language, Lorenzo Valla already speaks of the death (or the near death) of the Latin letters that will now be reawakened to new life (*ac paene cum litteris ipsis demortuae, hoc tempore excitentur ac reviviscant*).

Many years later, when the humanist discussion, starting with Bembo, took the form of a "debate about language" (*questione della lingua*) and a contrast between vernacular humanism and Latin humanism, it would be precisely the idea of the death of language—an idea originally forged for the sake of vindicating Latin—that would furnish arms to the proponents of the vernacular. In Sperone Speroni's *Dialogo delle lingue* (which dates from 1542, thus more than 40 years after *Hypnerotomachia* and almost 20 years after *Prose della volgar lingua*), the growth and death of Latin are a natural phenomenon, comparable to the vital cycle of a plant: "For this is the will of nature, who has decided that this tree soon be born, flower, and bear fruit, and that another soon grow old and die." The vernacular, by contrast, is a "virgin" who has not yet fully flowered: "I tell you that this modern language, however old it is, is still quite a young and delicate virgin, one who has not yet fully flowered and borne the fruits of which she is capable." On the lips of the courtier who is the spokesman for the vernacular, the superiority of the vernacular over Latin is by now simply the superiority of the living over the dead: "May you be permitted to want to hold it [the Latin language] in your mouths dead as it is; and leave us idiots in peace to speak our living vernaculars with the tongue that God gave us."[9]

Once Bembo's claims had won their battle, the concepts of dead language and living language appeared in Varchi's *Ercolana*, 70 years after *Hypnerotomachia*, as the accepted instruments of linguistic classification that are perfectly familiar to us ("Of languages, some are living and some are not living. The non-living languages are of two kinds: those which we would call wholly dead, and those which are half alive"). At the same time, the problem of whether the vernacular is "a new language on its own or merely the ancient language, now broken and corrupted"—a problem that had been greatly debated among the humanists—was resolved in favor of a relative but firm autonomy of the vernacular ("thus this language will be considered to be new, though built on the foundations of Latin").[10] The first generations of humanists had been so convinced of the vernacular's substantial difference from Latin that they claimed the vernacular could have derived etymologically from Latin only through the mediation of Greek or a barbarian language. Now these very ideas, which had been used to support the superiority of Latin, are instead invoked to justify the excellence of the vernacular.

Dionisotti has justly observed that modern historians have too often and too easily tried to explain the passage from Latin humanism to vernacular humanism as the normal outcome of a conflict between a dead language and a living language.[11] A simple glance at the dates of the texts cited demonstrates that in the years in which *Hypnerotomachia* was written, the idea of the death of language had not yet acquired its modern meaning, which emerges only in functional proximity to the polemic against Latin. This does not mean that the idea of a dead language was not yet present, but only that it did not retain the same meaning before and after the watershed marked by *Prose della volgar lingua*. Before *Prose della volgar lingua*, the idea of a dead language was the condition of a rebirth and restoration; afterward it marked the definite end of the spoken use of Latin. If we want to verify the sense and truth of our identification of Polia as an old and dead language, we must therefore attempt to reckon precisely with this difference and to enter a zone in which the crisis of language between the fifteenth and sixteenth centuries had not yet assumed the form—a form that is so determining for the Italian tradition—of a "debate about language."

V

To measure the novelty of the idea of Latin as a dead language, it is necessary to stress the break that it marked with respect to fourteenth-century ideas. In Dante's *Convivio* and *De vulgari eloquentia*, the perishable and dead language par excellence is still the vernacular, while Latin is "perpetual and incorruptible." Insofar as it is the *lingua grammatica*, Latin is, for Dante, what puts an end to the mortality of languages. The fact of the matter is that Dante's bilingualism and the bilingualism of the fifteenth and sixteenth centuries in no way refer to the same phenomenon. The first corresponds to the opposition not so much between two languages as between two different experiences of language, which Dante calls the mother tongue and the grammatical language. The vernacular is an absolutely primordial and immediate experience of speech ("first speech" [*prima locutio*] [*De vulgari eloquentia*, I, 2, 21]; "[it is] one and only in the mind; that which is alone and first in the whole mind" [*uno e solo è prima nella mente; quello che è solo prima in tutta la mente*] [*Convivio*, I, XIII, 5]). It is an experience prior not only to all other languages but also to all science and all knowledge, of which it constitutes the necessary condition ("this vernacular of mine was what led me into the path of knowledge which is our ultimate perfection, since through it I entered upon Latin and through its agency Latin was taught to me" [*Questo mio volgare fi introduttore di me ne la via della scienza, che è ultima perfezione, in quanto con esso io entrai ne lo latino e con esso mi fu mostrato*] [*Convivio*, I, XIII, 5]).[12] This primordiality of the vernacular—which is truly something like the dwelling of the *logos* in the beginning of Johanine theology—is, Dante says, "a cause that engenders love" (*cagione d'amore generativa*), that is, the ground of the "most perfect love of one's own language" (*perfettissimo amore alla propria loquela*), which is so important for him. And yet, for all its primordiality, precisely because it coincides immediately with the illumination of the mind that gives rise to knowledge and because it experiences the "ineffability" (*ineffabilitade*) (*Convivio*, III, IV, 1) implicit in this illumination, the vernacular can follow only "use," not "art"; and it is, therefore, necessarily transient and subject to continual death. To speak in the vernacular is precisely to experience this incessant death and rebirth of words, which no grammar can fully treat. (This is why Dante says, in *Convivio*, II, XIII, 10, that "the rays of reason" [*li raggi de la ragione*] cannot "end" [*terminarsi*] in language, "in particular in words" [*in parte spezialmente de li vocaboli*]; in fact, "certain words, certain declensions, and certain constructions are now in use which formerly were not, and many were formerly in use which will yet be in use again" [*certi vocaboli, certe declinazioni, certe costruzioni sono in uso che già non furono, e molto già furono che ancor saranno*]).[13]

The *lingua grammatica* is instead the language of knowledge, *locutio secundaria*. Grammatical language always presupposes the mother tongue and can be learned, by means of rules and study, only through the mother tongue. This is why grammatical language is unalterable and perpetual (hence the apparent contradiction according to which the greater nobility of Latin does not exclude the primogeniture of the vernacular).

Dante's reflections on Latin and the vernacular must be situated in the context of this double experience of speech, which was possible only in the brief period between the appearance of the literary consciousness of the vernacular in the love poets and the construction of the first grammars in Romance languages (*Las leys d'amors* dates from the first decades of the fourteenth century, and *Donat proensal* appeared earlier; but Italian grammar emerged with Fortunio's *Regole* in 1516). Only if considered in this light can Dante's project be understood: to give stability to the vernacular, which is constituted as the language of poetry, without transforming it into a grammatical language.

The bilingualism of the fifteenth and sixteenth centuries, by contrast, presupposes a regulated and instrumental relation to language that is substantially the same for both Latin and the vernacular. The struggle between Ciceronian Latin and the fourteenth-century vernacular as Bembo understood it was, from Dante's point of view, a struggle between two grammatical languages: both renounce the primordial experience of the event of language; both seem to presuppose a knowledge and a prelinguistic thought that, as has been suggested for the Latin thinkers of the late Middle Ages, might coincide with the vernacular, which is singularly obscured in debates about language. The crisis of language that took place between the fifteenth and the sixteenth centuries was therefore not simply the contrast between a dead (or half living) language and a living language that naturally succeeds it. (As the more lucid thinkers immediately realized, even the fourteenth-century vernacular proposed by Bembo was, after all, a dead language, a language that, in Bernardo Davanzati's words, "one does not speak, but learns like dead languages through the works of three Florentine writers.") Rather, the fifteenth- and sixteenth-century crisis of language marks the definitive decline of the experience from which Romance lyric poetry emerged, as well as a radical change in the nature of bilingualism.

In a decisive turning-point in European culture, Dante's antithesis between the vernacular and grammar—that is, between the experience of the originary and secondary status of the event of language (or, again, between *love* of language and *knowledge* of language)—therefore comes to be replaced by the antithesis between living language and dead language. The humanist opposition then conceals and, in fact, even overturns the meaning of the earlier distinction. For the essential bilingualism of human speech is now resolved through a diachronic separation by which one language is pushed backward, as "dead," prior to "living" language. Yet the language that thus dies—Latin—is not Dante's imperishable grammatical language but rather a mother tongue of a new kind, which is already the *lingua matrix* of seventeenth-century philology—the original language from which other languages derive and whose death renders possible the intelligibility and grammaticality of other languages. Only the appearance of Latin as a dead language allowed the vernacular to be transformed into a grammatical language. And it was precisely the idea of a dead language that, in the hands of

Romantic linguistics, made possible the birth of the modern science of language. For what is Indo-European—whose reconstruction marked the culmination of modern comparative grammar—if not the idea of a dead language that is always necessarily presupposed for every language and that, present precisely in being dead, sustains the systematic kinship and intelligibility of languages?

From this point of view, it can be said that the first generations of humanism, which passionately experienced the corruption and rebirth of Latin, transferred to Latin precisely the experience of language that had originally been the experience of the vernacular. Latin thus rose up again in humanism in a radically new form: it was now no longer the immobile grammatical language of the Middle Ages but rather a living and, by that token, corruptible and mortal language. The intellectual movement that captured this new experience of language was not Ciceronian humanism but rather the current of humanistic philology that, from Poliziano to Beroaldo to Pio, had concentrated its lexicographic attention on the archaic and late *facies* of the latinity that was soon to be rigidified into a canon following the victory of Bembo's position. In the praxis of this seemingly pedantic philology, in its obsessive excavations of obsolete and rare words, Latin was not an instrumental language (whether alive or dead) but an experience in which what was incessantly at play was—as in the vernacular love poets—death and rebirth. Only by recuperating this linguistic problematic in all its complexity is it possible to situate the language of *Hypnerotomachia* in its real context. And it is from this perspective that we must now look to what is certainly one of this work's most singular intentions: its abandonment of the vernacular in favor of a humanist lexical passion, together with its retrieval of moments and contents that fourteenth-century love poetry had assigned precisely to the vernacular.

VI

The affinities between Polifilo's tale of love and the themes of the Dolce Stil Novo and Dante's lyric poetry have been often noted. "Polifilo and Polia" have been said to be "like Dante and Beatrice," and it has been pointed out how, under her fifteenth-century robes, Polia continues the soteriological function of the lady in lyric poetry, even as Polifilo is "humble and trembling like the lovers of the Dolce Stil Novo."[14] And it is precisely the text's solid reference to love poetry and consequent retrieval of the Dolce Stil Novo feminine figure that allows us to verify and deepen our hypothesis concerning Polia. For just as Polifilo's unique linguistic practice implicitly contains a reflection on language, so behind the Provençal and Dolce Stil Novo theory of love stands a radical reflection on poetic language. This reflection is, in fact, so new and important that only the pseudoscientific hermeneutic tradition that has for centuries obstinately searched for referential information beyond textual elements could have obscured it.

The significance of what appears in the poetic text as a feminine name and figure has been distorted by the seemingly thoughtless gesture with which Boccaccio, reporting what appeared to be a piece of local gossip, identified Beatrice with the daughter of Folco Portinari, later wife of Simone de' Bardi. The meaning of this gesture, which was already accomplished in the germinal short stories that are Provençal *vidas* and *razos*, can be grasped only if it is understood in strict solidarity with Boccaccio's creation of the Florentine novella. For the Provençals as for the Dolce Stil Novo poets, the experience of love was the experience of the absolute primacy of the event of words over life and of *what is poeticized* [*il poetato*] over *what is lived* [*il vissuto*]. Now this experience is overturned in the idea that every poeticization is, instead, always a poeticization of life, a putting into words—*narration*—of a biographical event. If one looks closely, however, both Boccaccio and the anonymous authors of the troubadour *vidas* do nothing other than follow the love poets' intention through to its most extreme consequence. Constructing a biographical anecdote to explain a poem, they invent *what is lived* on the basis of *what is poeticized*, and not vice versa. If Dante's experience of the absolute originarity of speech was a "new life," even as in John's Gospel it is said that what is made in the word is life, then in a certain sense Beatrice truly was a Florentine girl.

Boccaccio himself suggests that his remark is in no case to be read merely biographically and referentially. Responding in a sonnet to the accusation of having revealed the mysteries of poetry to the uninitiated, he writes:

> Io ho messo in galea senza biscotto
> l'ingrato vulgo, et senza alcun piloto
> lasciato l'ho in mar a lui non noto,
> benché sen creda esser maestro e dotto.
>
> (I put the ungrateful vulgar in a ship
> without biscuit, and left them without
> any pilot on a sea that they knew not,
> although they think themselves masters
> and men of learning.)[15]

Having repeated the tale of Bice Portinari for five centuries, scholars of Italian literature, the ungrateful vulgar, continue to drift aimlessly at sea, although they think themselves masters and men of learning. It is therefore time to reveal what every intelligent scholar has always known, explicitly or implicitly: Beatrice is the name of the amorous experience of the event of language at play in the poetic text itself. She is thus the name and the love of language, but of language understood not in its grammaticality but, rather, in its radical primordiality, as the emergence of verse from the pure Nothing (*de dreit nien*, according to the *incipit* of Guilhem IX's *vers*). It is because of its absolute originarity that speech is the supreme cause and object of love and, at the same time, necessarily transient and perishable. Dante's essential experience of speech, Beatrice's death, and the loss of Edenic language narrated in the first book of *De vulgari eloquentia* acquire their full significance from this perspective. If Dante begins by seeking in poetic practice, and not grammar, to confer stability and duration on the vernacular, he ends, in the Comedy, by wholly accepting the irreparable loss of every mother tongue and by stating, through Adam, that even before the construction of the tower of Babel Edenic language was already "all extinct" (*tutta spenta*) (*Paradiso*, XXVI, 124–29).

In *Hypnerotomachia*, the demand for a primordial status and Edenic *vetustas* of speech is inserted not into the firm opposition between mother tongue and grammatical language but rather into a situation in which the vernacular is being transformed into a grammatical language and Latin is becoming a dead language. This is why *Hypnerotomachia*'s language cannot coherently be defined either as a mother tongue or as a grammatical language, either as a living language or as a dead language. It is, instead, all of these at once. Drastically reducing all these different levels of bilingualism into one single plane, *Hypnerotomachia* presents language as a battlefield between irreconcilable demands. According to the model of lyric poetry, however, this battle is an amorous fight, a combat of eros (*erotomachia*) that gives rise to a reciprocal estrangement and incessant exchange of life and death between Latin and the vernacular. In Provençal and Dolce Stil Novo poetry, the "dispute" was that poetic form in which different mother tongues, in their Babelic dispersion, were called to bear witness to the love of the one distant language. In this sense, *Hypnerotomachia* is a dispute of the most novel kind, in which different languages are penetrated by each other, thus revealing every language's intimate discord with itself, the bilingualism implicit in all human speech.

At this point, can we still see in Polia—the old language—simply a figure for Latin? Here an additional hint can be found in a work that the author often consulted, as shown by the texts collected by Pozzi and Ciapponi. In Isidore of Seville's *Etymologiae* (IX, I, 6), medieval thought, uniting its early historical consciousness with a metahistorical consideration of linguistic facts, distinguished four ages or figures of the Latin language. In Isidore's list, the first receives the name of Prisca, "the disordered language that was used, in a disordered state, by the most ancient Italians under Janus and Saturn, as when they had the poems of the Salii" (*quam vetustissimi Italiae sub Iano et Saturno sunt usi, incondita, ut se habent carmina saliorum*). Prisca, the ancient woman, is Latin, but she is Latin not as a language of knowledge but rather as an unknown language of the Golden Age, a language equivalent to the pre-Babelic language of the biblical tradition said to have survived in fragments of poems belonging to the Salii, the priests of Mars. The figure of Polia is certainly tied to the experience of this unformed, originary dimension of language through the allegedly pedantic practice of humanist philology. But at the same time, through its position in the vernacular culture, Polia and Polifilo's love can become a figure for the pure self-referentiality of language. The object sought by love would then coincide with the very language in which the book is written. As we have seen, this language—Polia, the old woman—is neither Latin nor the vernacular, neither a dead language nor a living language, but—if the book is a dream—a dreamt language, the dream of an unknown and absolutely novel language whose existence lies in its textual reality alone. In the phrase "dream of language," the genitive "of" certainly has an objective value (in the sense that here an unknown language is dreamt); but it also has a subjective or possessive value if the book is made by Polia herself, as the dedication suggests. (And, after all, does not every dream imply a problem of bilingualism? Is the dream not always a dimension not *beyond* languages but *between* them and, as such, in need of an interpretation and a *Deutung*?)

In this perfect self-referentiality, the book fully realizes—if only through its unique bilingualism—the project attempted by Dante and the Dolce Stil Novo poets in their poetry: to present the absolute dwelling of language in the beginning. With the disappearance of its originary opposition to grammar, Dante's language, Beatrice, entered into the linguistic history in which we still move today, even if this entry took place through a number of misunderstandings. Yet after five centuries, Polia remains unfamiliar, as dead and inextinguishable in her closed dream as she was at the moment in which her author—whoever he may have been—consigned her to the leaves of his incunabulum. But this dream, which is fully contemporary today, is in fact dreamt again every time a text, restoring the bilingualism and discord implicit in every language, seeks to evoke the pure language that, while absent in every instrumental language, makes human speech possible. (Instances of such texts are numerous even in recent Italian literary history, from Giovanni Pascoli's use of obsolete and foreign words to Carlo

Emilio Gadda's neologisms and archaisms and the increasing intrusion of dialect into the body of language.)

The dream of the old woman—the dream of language—lasts to this day. How we might wake from it in the end, how we, the speaking beings, might awaken from the dream of language and once and for all leave behind us the illusion of bilingualism—whether, in other words, there can be human speech that is univocal and withdrawn from all bilingualism—these questions lie beyond the scope of this essay. Here we have restricted ourselves to the subject indicated by the name of the conference, "Languages of Dreaming."

§ 4 Pascoli and the Thought of the Voice

To Gianfranco Contini

I

Gianfranco Contini was the first to identify in Giovanni Pascoli's poetics an aspiration to work in a dead language that exceeded his poetic craftsmanship in Latin. Following the ambition that is common to all great European decadent poets (but that has perhaps a stronger lineage in Italy) to write in a new language, Pascoli, Contini argues, positioned himself in relation to language as to a "reserve of poetic objects that were once alive and to which life was to be restored." Hence his appropriation in normal language of special languages ("down to those extremely special ones that are the phonic sequences of proper names"); hence too his obstinate recourse to the agrammatical or pregrammatical language of onomatopoeia (the "insufferable presence of birds" that so bothered Pintor). It would be superfluous to reaffirm the precision of this diagnosis here. Instead we observe that Contini could also have cited a text of Pascoli's in which the poetics of a dead language is explicitly formulated as such. In a passage of *Pensieri scolastici*, polemicizing against the proposal to abolish the instruction of Greek in schools, Pascoli writes, "the language of poets is always a dead language," and immediately adds, "a curious thing—a dead language used to give greater life to thought."

We wish to depart from this last sentence, continuing to reflect on the relation between poetry and dead language in order to interrogate Pascoli's poetry in a dimension in which what is at issue is no longer simply his poetics but his dictation: the dictation of poetry, if we mean by this term (which we take from the vocabulary of medieval poetics, but which has never ceased to be familiar to the Italian poetic tradition) the experience of the originary event of speech itself. Poetry, Pascoli says, speaks in a dead language; but dead language is what gives life to thought. Thought lives off the death of words. From this perspective, to think and to poeticize is to experience the death of speech, to utter (and to resuscitate) dead words. Contini observes that the problem of the death of words troubled Pascoli as much as the death of creatures. But in what way and in what sense can a dead language give life to thought? In what way can poetry accomplish this experience of dead words? And what—since this is what is at issue—is a dead word?

II

In a passage of *De Trinitate* that constitutes one of the first places in which the idea of a dead language appears, St. Augustine offers a meditation on a dead word, a *vocabulum emortuum*. Let us suppose, he says, that someone hears an unknown sign, the sound of a word of whose meaning he is ignorant, for example the word *temetum* (an obsolete term for *vinum*). Being ignorant of the word's meaning, he will certainly want to know it. But for this it is necessary that he already know that the sound he has heard is not an empty voice (*inanem vocem*), the mere sound *te-me-tum*, but rather a signifying sound. Otherwise that trisyllabic sound will already be fully known the moment it is perceived:

> When all its letters and the length of each sound are known, what else would there be in it to look for to know it better, if one did not also know that it is a sign, and if one were not moved by the desire to know what it signified? The more the word is registered, without being fully so, the more the soul therefore desires to know that residue of knowledge. If it knew only the existence of this voice and not that it signified something, the soul would have nothing to search for

once it had perceived the sensible sound as best it could. But since the soul already knows that there is not only a voice but also a sign, it wants to have perfect knowledge of it. Can one say that someone is without love if, with ardent zeal, he seeks to know and perseveres, excited by his studies? Can one say that he therefore loves? Certainly it is not possible to love something that is not known. And he does not love these three syllables that he already knows. Can it then be said that what he loves in them is the knowledge that they signify something?

In this passage, the experience of the dead word appears as the experience of a word uttered (a *vox*) insofar as it is no longer mere sound (*istas tres syllabas*), but not yet a signification—insofar as it is the experience, that is, of a sign as pure meaning [*voler-dire*] and intention to signify before and beyond the arrival of every particular signification. For Augustine, this experience of an unknown word (*verbum ignotum*) in the no-man's-land between sound and signification is the experience of love as will to know. What corresponds to the intention to signify without signification is not logical understanding, in fact, but rather the desire to know (*qui scire amat incognita, non ipsa incognita, sed ipsum scire amat*: love is thus always the desire to know). It is important, however, to stress that the site of this experience of love, which shows the *vox* in its purity, is a dead word, a *vocabulum emortuum*: *temetum*.

(Let us note here, in passing, that the Provençal and Dolce Stil Novo theory of love can only be understood as an attempt to call into question this very passage in Augustine. *Amor de lonh* is precisely the wager that there can be love that never passes into knowledge, an *amare ipsa incognita*, that is, a word—here too a word that is, not by chance, obscure and rare: *cars, bruns e tenhz motz*—that can never be translated into the logical experience of signification.)

III

In the eleventh century, medieval logic returned, even before poetry did, to the Augustinian experience of the unknown voice to ground in it the most universal and originary experience, that of Being. In his objection to St. Anselm's ontological argument, Gaunilo affirms the possibility of an experience of thought that neither signifies nor refers to a *res*, but instead dwells in "the voice alone." Reformulating the Augustinian experiment, he proposes a thinking that conceives

> not so much the voice itself, which is something somehow true, that is, the sound of the syllables and letters, so much as the signification of the voice that is heard; not, however, as it is conceived by him who knows what is usually signified by that voice, but rather as it is conceived by him who does not know its signification and thinks only according to the movement of the soul, which seeks to represent the signification of the voice that is perceived.

No longer mere sound and not yet logical signification, this "thought of the voice alone" (*cogitatio secundum vocem solam*) opens thought to an unheard dimension sustained in the pure breath of the voice, in mere *vox* as insignificant will to signify.

IV

In 1 Corinthians 14:1–25, Paul expresses his stubborn critique of the linguistic practice of the Christian community of Corinth:

> He that speaketh in an unknown tongue [*ho lalon glosse, qui loquitur lingua*, according to St. Jerome] speaketh not unto men, but unto God: for no man understandeth him; howbeit in the spirit he speaketh mysteries. . . . He that speaketh in an unknown tongue edifieth himself; but he that prophesieth edifieth the church. . . . Now, brethren, if I come unto you speaking with tongues, what shall I profit you, except I shall speak to you either by revelation, or by knowledge, or by prophesying, or by doctrine? . . . So likewise ye, except ye utter by the tongue words easy to be understood, how shall it be known what is spoken? For ye shall speak into the air. . . . If I know not the meaning of the voice, I shall be unto him that speaketh a barbarian, and he that speaketh shall be a barbarian unto me. . . . Wherefore let him that speaketh in an unknown tongue pray that he may not interpret. For if I pray in an unknown tongue, my spirit prayeth, but my understanding is unfruitful. . . . Brethren, be not children in understanding.

How are we to understand the text's *lalon glosse*? New Testament hermeneutics has established that *glossa* means "speech foreign to the language of use; obscure term, whose meaning is not understood." This is the meaning the word already had in Aristotle; but Quintilian still speaks of *glossemata* as *voces minus usitatae* ("more unusual sounds"), which belong to the "more mysterious language, which the Greeks call *glossas*" (*lingua secretior, quam Graeci glossas vocant*). *Glossolalia* is therefore not the pure utterance of inarticulate sounds but rather a "speech in glosses," that is, a speech whose meaning is unknown, exactly like Augustine's *temetum*. If I do not know the word's *dynamis* (this too is a grammatical term, one which means "semantic value"), Paul says, I will be a barbarian with respect to the person to whom I speak, and he who speaks in me shall be a barbarian. The expression "he that speaketh in me" (*ho lalon en emoi*) poses a problem that the Vulgate and the King James Bible resolve in interpreting *en emoi* as *mihi*, "for me," "unto me." But the text's *en emoi* can only signify "in me," and what Paul means is perfectly clear: if I utter words whose meaning I do not understand, he who speaks in me, the voice that utters them, the very principle of speech in me, will be something barbarous, something that does not know how to speak and that does not know what it says. To-speak-in-gloss is thus to experience in oneself barbarian speech, speech that one does not know; it is to experience an "infantile" speech ("Brethren, be not children in understanding") in which understanding is "unfruitful."

V

What, for Pascoli, is the experience of dead language as the "language of the poets"? Is it possible also to find in his poetry a dimension of language that, appearing with the characteristics we have sketched for the "thought of the voice alone" and for *glossolalia*, has its place between the withdrawal of mere sound and the arrival of signification? And if this were the case, would it then be possible to interpret in a new way and, at the same time, to grasp the unity of Pascoli's poetics of dead language, his onomatopoetics and his phono-symbolism? We continue to stand before Pascoli's text as "barbarians" who do not know the *dynamis* of words. "There are little words that are poorly understood" and that, despite the glossary that closes (and does not open!) *Canti di Castelvecchio,* do not truly want to be interpreted and to depart from the pure intention to signify that characterizes speaking in gloss. Contini has already noted the purely phono-symbolic value of the word "zillano" in "L'amorosa giornata." But this observation could be extended to the terms "schilletta," "sericcia," "accia," "gronchio," "grasce," "stiglie," "astile," "palestrita," "stiampa," "sprillo," "tarmolo," "strino," "legoro," "cuccolo," "guaime," and innumerable other glosses, as in the xenoglossiae of "Italy" and "The Hammerless Gun" (these last disseminated among ornithological onomatopoeias).

Pascoli counts on a reader who does not know all the words he uses. As the "poet of a dead language" says, in a text that bears that name, poetry, like religion, needs "words that veil and darken their meaning, words, I mean, foreign to present use" (and which are nevertheless used "to give greater life to thought"). *Glossalalia* and *xenoglossia* are the ciphers of the death of language: they represent language's departure from its semantic dimension and its return to the original sphere of the pure intention to signify (not mere sound, but rather language and thought of the voice alone). Thought and language, we would say today, of pure phonemes— for what else can it mean to note an intention to signify that is distinct from mere sound but that does not yet signify, if not to recognize language's phonemes, the negative and purely differential entities that according to modern linguistics have no signification and, at the same time, make signification possible?

It is therefore not truly a matter of phono-symbolism, but rather a matter of a sphere so to speak beyond or before sound, a sphere that does not *symbolize* anything as much as it simply *indicates* an intention to signify, that is, the voice in its originary purity. This is an indication that has its place neither in mere sound nor in signification but rather, we might say, in pure *grammata*, in pure letters, precisely like the "black sowing" of language that, in *Myricae*'s "Piccolo aratore," later flowers into a sonorous and living world, or like those very letters that, gathered in "mantelle" (another gloss!), in *Piccolo mietitore* speak between one's teeth, "like us, but better than us."

VI

Analogous observations can be made for Pascoli's onomatopoeias, for those "siccecé," "uid," "videvitt," "scilp," "zisteretet," "trr trr terit," "fru," "sii sii," "scricchiolettii," "frulli," and "sgrigiolii" that crowd the verses of *Canti* and *Myricae* and that the poet himself, speaking of the language of swallows, assimilates to a dead language "no longer known." Onomatopoeia is generally characterized as a pregrammatical or agrammatical language ("this language," Contini writes, "as such has nothing to do with grammar"). In the introduction to his *Principles of Phonology*, N. S. Trubetskoy, considering the vocal imitation of natural sounds, writes: "If someone tells a hunting story and, to enliven his tale, imitates an animal sound or any other natural noise, he must at that point *interrupt* his story; the natural sound imitated is then a foreign body that remains outside normal representative discourse."

Yet is it certain that Pascoli's onomatopoeias are a pregrammatical language? And what, first of all, is a "pregrammatical" language? Is such a language—a dimension of human language that is altogether not grammatical—even conceivable?

Ancient grammarians began their studies with the voice (*phone*). But the voice, as pure natural sound, did not enter into grammar. Grammar above all begins by distinguishing the "confused voice" of animals (*phone agrammatos*; the Latins translate this as *vox illiterata, quae litteris comprehendi non potest*, which cannot be written, like the *equorum hinnitus* and the *rabies canum*) from the human voice, which can be written (*engrammatos*) and articulated. A more subtle classification, which is of Stoic origin, nevertheless characterizes the voice with greater sophistication. "One must know," we read in Dionysius Thrace's *Techne grammatike*,

> that among voices, some are articulate and capable of being written [*engrammatoi*], like ours. Others, such as the crackling of fire and the

din of stone and wood, are inarticulate and cannot be written. Others still, such as imitations of irrational animals, like *brekekeks* and *koi*, are inarticulate and yet can be written; these voices are inarticulate, since we do not know what they mean, but they are *engrammatoi*, since they can be written.

Let us pause to consider these inarticulate and yet "writable" voices, these *brekekeks* and *koi*, which are so similar to Pascoli's onomatopoeias. What happens to the confused animal voice such that it becomes *engrammatos* and comprehended by letters? In entering into *grammata* in being written, the animal voice is separated from nature, which is inarticulate and cannot be written; it shows itself in letters as a pure intention to signify whose signification is unknown (it is in this respect similar to *glossolalia* and Augustine's *vocabulum emortuum*). The only criterion that makes it possible to distinguish it from the articulated voice is, in fact, that "we do not know what it means." The *gramma*, the letter, which itself does not signify, is therefore the cipher of an intention to signify that will be accomplished in articulated language. *Brekekeks, koi,* and other imitations of animal voices capture the voice of nature at the point at which it emerges from the infinite sea of mere sound without yet having become signifying discourse.

It is in light of these considerations that we must regard Pascoli's onomatopoeias. It is not a matter of mere natural sounds that simply interrupt articulated discourse; in Pascoli's poetry, as in every human language, there is no—and there could never be—presence of the animal voice. There is, rather, only a trace of the animal voice's absence, of its "death," which renders itself grammatical in a pure intention to signify. Like Caprona's "schilletta" (in *Canti di Castelvecchio*), these sounds belong to no living being; they are a bell hanging on the neck of a "shadow," a dead animal that now continues to sound between the hands of a "little boy" who "does not speak." The voice, as in the poem by this name in *Canti*, is noted only "at the point in which it dies," as an intention to signify ("to say many things and still more") which as such cannot say and signify anything other than the "breath" of a proper name ("Zvani"). From this perspective, the *dead voice* is certainly equivalent to the swallows' *dead language* in "Addio"—a language that is not pregrammatical, however, but rather purely and absolutely grammatical in the most rigorous and originary sense of the word: *phone engrammatos, vox litterata.*

VII

The letter is therefore the dimension in which *glossolalia* and onomatopoeia, the poetics of dead language and the poetics of the dead voice, converge in one site, where Pascoli situates the most proper experience of poetic dictation: *the site in which he can capture language in the instant it sinks again, dying, into the voice, and at which the voice, emerging from mere sound, passes (that is, dies) into signification.* In Pascoli's poetry, *glossolalia* and onomatopoeia speak from one and the same place, even if they seem to pass through it in opposite directions. Hence the exemplary character of the verses in which onomatopoeia crosses over into articulated language and articulated language crosses over into onomatopoeia:

> Finch . . . finchè nel cielo volai
> V'è di voi chi vide . . . vide . . . videvitt
> Anch'io anch'io chio chio chio.

> (Unt . . . until I flew in the sky, there
> were those among you who saw . . .
> saw . . . sawitt. Me too me too eetoo
> eetoo eetoo eetoo.)

Hence also the particular status in Pascoli's poetry of the proper name, whose sphere of signification poses almost insurmountable problems for linguistics, and which Roman Jakobson says does not have proper signification, being simply a reference of the linguistic code to itself. At the limit between onomatopoeia and *glossolalia*, the proper name seems to constitute a dark point of crossing between voice and language. If "Zvani" is the "breath" of the voice "at the point at which it dies," in "Lapide" the proper name inscribed on the tomb of a girl is explicitly defined as the "thought" that the living being, dying, exhales into language:

> Lascia argentei il cardo al leggero
> tuo alito i pappi suoi come
> il morente alla morte un pensiero
> vago, ultimo: l'ombra di un nome.

> (The thistle leaves its silver pappi to
> your light breath, as the dying man
> leaves a thought to death a vague,
> last thought: the shadow of a name.)

Consider also the onomastic series of "Gog e Magog," which recalls the Babelic language of Dante's Nemrod:

> di Mong, Mosach, Thubal, Aneg, Ageg,
> Assur, Pothim, Cephar, Alan, a me!

> (Mong, Mosach, Thubal, Aneg, Ageg,
> Assur, Pothim, Cephar, Alan, to me!)

Here the pure language of names, in which the dead voice is inscribed, decays and cannot be separated from the *glossolalia* of words that "veil and darken their meaning."

The experience of this "crossing over," which constitutes the site of Pascoli's poetic dictation, is an experience of death. It is only in dying that the animal voice is, in the letter, destined to enter signifying language as pure intention to signify; and it is only in dying that articulated language can return to the indistinct womb of the voice from which it originated. Poetry is the experience of the letter, but the letter has its place in death: in the death of the voice (onomatopoeia) or the death of language (*glossolalia*), the two of which coincide in the brief flash of *grammata*.

VIII

In this context we can also better understand the theory of the "little boy" (*fanciullino*) by which Pascoli tried to capture his own experience of poetry in terms of a dictation (the little boy "dictated inside" [*detta dentro*] like love in Dante). If the reader often confronts Pascoli's text like the Pauline barbarian who does not know the *dynamis* of words, the claim that genuinely characterizes Pascoli's experience of dictation is that "he that speaketh" in the poet is also a barbarian, speaking without knowing what he says and thus uttering speech in its inceptive state, as pure intention to signify and the language of names. In accordance with these principles, the dictation of the little boy is mainly presented in terms of voice ("he confuses his voice with ours . . . he feels only a palpitation, a screeching and a howling . . . like the ringing of a bell . . . hearing its chattering").[1] And the little boy appears as "Adam, who was the first to give names." What is decisive, however, is that in the "Ritorno a san Mauro" poems that close *Canti*, his figure is revealed as the figure of a tomb, the shaded profile of a dead person that fades away and at times almost merges with that other dead person, his mother. All the "Ritorno a san Mauro" poems are greatly clarified if they are read as a dialogue with a dead language (the mother) and a dead voice (the little boy), which now betray their secret unity. In "Mia madre," the infantile voice remains near the dead mother:

> Tra i pigolii dei nidi
> io vi sentii la voce
> mia di fanciullo.
>
> (In the chirping of
> the nests, I heard
> my voice, the voice
> of a little boy.)

And in "Giovannino," the little boy inhabits the limit of the cemetery, being by now in his poetic function clearly equivalent to the maternal figure. It is this vision of the grave that lies at the center of the poem in which Pascoli most successfully captured his own experience of dictation: "La tessitrice" ("The Seamstress"), which, in a dialogue between the poet and a voice, takes hold of the awful event of the poetic word.

Here, at the heart of the dictation, there was not even "the sound of one word"; the loom that weaves the cloth of language "no longer . . . sounds" and everything is only "mute gesture." Only af-

ter the question "Why does it not sound?" is repeated twice does
the vocal virgin (little boy and muse, voice and maternal language)
reveal her own irreparable death:

> E piange e piange—Mio dolce amore,
> non t'hanno detto? non lo sai tu?
> Io non son viva che nel tuo cuore.
>
> Morta! Sì, morta! Se tesso, tesso
> per te soltanto.
>
> (And cry, and cry. My sweet love, did
> they not tell you? Do you not know it?
> I am alive only in your heart. Dead!
> Yes, dead! If I weave, I weave for you
> alone.)

"La tessitrice" thus says the truth that *Il fanciullino* still kept veiled:
the little boy does not exist, and the infantile voice dictating poetry is a dead voice, just as only a dead voice captures its dictation.
(Hence the inadequacy of the criticisms so often leveled at *Il fanciullino*, which supposedly "confused the little boy nature and the
little boy poetry": what is at issue here is not simply a "voice of nature" or a poetic determination but rather the purely negative relation between the living being and nature in which voice and language become indistinct in death.) We can consider this trait as
one of those that most deeply marks the physiognomy of Italian
culture: the will and the consciousness of operating in a dead language, in an individual and artificially constructed language, which
is "glossolalic" in the sense considered, with or without a "prayer
of interpretation." Here we must think not only of those names
that immediately come to mind when thinking of twentieth-
century Italian writers—Gadda and Montale, Pasolini, Noventa,
Zanzotto—but also of those prose writers who work in an apparently different area, such as Longhi, whose use of the word "scan-
delle" ("drops or particles of light") in his essay on Serodine makes
his syntax reminiscent of Pascoli. Such is this people's difficult and
enigmatic relation to their mother tongue, by which it can only
find itself in it if it succeeds in hearing it as dead, and by which it

can only love it and make it its own in breaking it into fragments and anatomical segments. Here, too, Beatrice's death conditions Italy's entire literary tradition, and Petrarch's Laura (aura, "l'aura") is nothing but the breath of the voice—a voice that, in the end, is only "dead air," *aura morta.*

IX

For Pascoli, human language is therefore always "language that no longer sounds on the lips of the living" in the double sense that it is necessarily a dead language or a dead voice and it is never the living voice of man or the speech of any living creature. Pascoli, we might say, descends like Faust into the Reign of the Mothers, the goddesses who shelter "what has not existed for a long time" and in whom we must see a figure of mother tongues and Scaligero's *matrices linguae.* Like Faust, Pascoli discovers that the Mothers are dead, and that around their heads fly only images that are "mobile, but lifeless" (even if it is possible, through song, to animate them and to make them sing). And the voice of nature is unattainable and dead along with them. (And is it not perhaps true that our every word is a "dead letter," a dead language handed down to us by the dead, which can never give rise to something living? How is it possible, then, for these lifeless words to become our living voice, for dead letters to sing suddenly in the heart of the poet?)

To speak, to poeticize, to think can only be, from this perspective, to experience the letter as the experience of the death of one's own language and one's own voice. Pascoli's experience of "letters" is so serious and extreme that this is what it means, for him, to be "a man of letters." Pascoli, "he who, when seen from behind, seemed a creator," who certainly wrote "a terrible amount of ugly poems," is therefore truly "the most European of Italian poets at the turn of the century." The poet of metaphysics in the age of its decline, Pascoli most radically experiences metaphysics' original mythologeme—the mythologeme of the voice, its death and memorial preservation in the letter.

This is precisely why, at the point at which we register the coherence and rigor of Pascoli's lesson, it is nevertheless necessary also to pose a question that must remain provisionally unanswered here: can there be an experience of speech that is not an experience of the letter in the sense that we have seen? Can there be speech, poetry, and thought beyond the letter, beyond the death of the voice and the death of language?

§ 5 The Dictation of Poetry

The problem of the relation between poetry and life has given rise to such tenacious ambiguities that it has justly fallen into disrepute. Claims for its legitimacy are, however, as ancient as the very definition of man as the "living being who has language." The problem's dubiousness coincides with the difficulties that this apparently trivial formula has never ceased to pose to thought. What does it mean for a living being to speak? Is language, as seems obvious, a creation and an expression of the living human being, or is the opposite true instead, as we are all too inclined to believe today? Do life and speech constitute an articulated unity, or is there a disjunction between the two that neither individual existence nor the historical development of humanity can overcome?

It is on this uneven ground that theology and, later, psychology and biology took up their residence. When literary criticism and aesthetics finally came to formulate the problem of the relation between lived experience and poeticized experience with regard to the work of art, the terrain on which the problem could have been correctly posed had already been covered over and forever altered.

II

It is of this territory that a summary stratigraphy should first of all be drawn. Excavation work in the direction indicated here is almost entirely lacking. From the perspective of the researcher, what ought to be the most proper site of the poetic work appears instead as a vast field partially submerged in psychological swampland, out of which imposing ruins and theological torsos occasionally rise. The lake-dwelling exiles of literary investigation are suspended on this uncertain terrain, almost without any contact with it. The structures of the literary work that the modern science of the text began to bring to light several decades ago do not, in the final analysis, delve into any other terrain. The fruitful work of analysis that it has undertaken has been possible only thanks to an *epochē* that has rigorously bracketed all elements of psychology and lived experience. What thus comes to the foreground of formalist criticism, however, is—without ever appearing consciously as such— a purely theological presupposition: the dwelling of the word in the beginning, of *logos* in *archē*, that is, the absolutely primordial status of language. This uninterrogated persistence of a theological foundation shows itself in the fact that the original structure of the poetic work remains marked by negativity: the primordiality of *logos* thus quickly becomes a primacy of the signifier and the letter, and the origin reveals itself as trace. (It is here that the deconstructionist factory establishes its residence.)

III

In the prologue to the Gospel of John, the interlacement of life (*zoē*) and speech (*logos*) is expressed in the following formula: "Everything was made by him [the Logos] and without him nothing of what was made was made. Life was in him, and life was the light of men." But until the fourth century, when the text was altered to combat the Arian heresy, and in the commentaries of the first Church Fathers and the Latin version that precedes the Vulgate, the text appeared in a different form, one that noticeably changes its meaning: "Everything was made by him, and without him nothing was made, and what was made in him was life, and life was the light of men." Commenting on these verses, the Gnostic Ptolomeus writes: "Everything was made by the Logos, but life was made *in* him. Life, which was made in him, is closer [*oikoiotera*] to him than what was made *by* him; life is one with him and bears fruit through him." In the same sense, Origen writes: "Life itself is made in coming to pass to language [*epiginetai toi logoi*] and, once made, remains inseparable [*akhoristos*] from him."

Life is what is made in speech and what remains indistinguishable from it and close to it. This unquestioned bond of speech and life is the inheritance that Christian theology transmits to a literature that has not yet become fully profane.

IV

In the theological tradition that emerges from the Johanine prologue, the life-language relation thus runs in precisely the opposite direction from the convention dominating the modern concept of biography. The theological tradition was so authoritative that it not only impeded the formation of a biographical canon in the modern sense but also determined how poets understood their relation to lived experience at the origins of Romance lyric poetry.

Ancient rhetoric gave the name *ratio* (or *ars*) *inveniendi* (as opposed to *ratio iudicandi*, which concerned the truth and correctness of spoken discourse) to the technique that allowed the orator or poet access to the place (hence the term *topica*) of speech, so that he might now and then find there the *argumentum* that he needed. Insofar as it sought above all to establish that the orator necessarily had at his disposal the "topics" he needed, ancient rhetoric in time decayed and became a mnemotechnics, conceiving of the "places" of speech as mnemonic images whose mastery assured the orator the ability to present his argument. The first germs of a mutation in this pagan conception of *inventio* following the new archetypal status of Johanine *logos* can already be found in St. Augustine's *De*

Trinitate, in which *inventio* is interpreted, by means of an etymological figure, as *in id venire quod queritur.* Man, that is, finds
speech only through an *appetitus,* an amorous desire, such that the
event of language appears as an inextricable interlacement of love,
speech, and knowledge. "While the mind loves itself and knows,
its word is joined to it through love. And since the mind loves
knowledge and knows love, speech is in love and love is in speech,
and both are in the lover and the speaker" (*cum itaque se mens novit
et amat, iungitur ei amore verbum eius. Et quoniam amat notitiam et
novit amorem, et verbum in amore et amor in verbo, et utrumque in
amante et dicente*).[1]

In the course of the twelfth century, topics and their *ratio inveniendi* were, in the wake of Augustine, interpreted in a radically
new way by the Provençal poets. Modern European lyric poetry has
its origin in this reinterpretation. For the poets, *ratio inveniendi* became *razo de trobar,* and it is from this expression that they drew
their own name (*trobador* and *trobaritz*). The new experience of
speech that is at issue here goes decisively back beyond classical *inventio*: the troubadours want not to recall arguments consigned to a
topos but instead to experience the very event of language as original
topos, which takes place in an absolute proximity of love, speech,
and knowledge. The *razo,* which lies at the foundation of poetry
and which constitutes what the poets call its dictation (*dictamen*), is
therefore neither a biographical nor a linguistic event. It is instead a
zone of indifference, so to speak, between lived experience and what
is poeticized [*il poetato*], an "experience of speech" as an inex-
haustible experience of love. *Amor* is the name given by the troubadours to this experience of the dwelling of speech in the beginning;
and for them love is therefore the *razo de trobar* par excellence.

V

Between the thirteenth and fourteenth centuries, the minstrels
and "scriveners" (so they define themselves in the Provençal song-
books they compile) Uc de Saint Circ and Miquel de la Tor com-
pose, in Provençal, the first examples of biography in Romance lit-

erature. A reversal of the poetry-life relation that defined the troubadours' poetic experience is accomplished in these germinal short
stories (some of which will appear in *Novellino*), which briefly relate the life of the troubadour and the episode that lay at the origin
of his poems. What for the troubadours was an *experience* of the
razo—that is, an experience of the event of language as love, as the
tight unity of what is lived and what is poeticized—now becomes a
giving of reasons for experience.

Yet things are not so simple. Take the *razo* of the famous song of
Bernart de Ventadorn, "Quan vei la lauzeta mover":

> And he [Bernart] presented himself to the duchess of Normandy, who
> was young and well understood honor, merit, and good words. And
> Bernart's verses pleased her very much, and she warmly welcomed him
> near her. He remained at her court in this way for a long time, and he
> fell in love with her and she fell in love with him, and he composed
> many beautiful songs. And he called her "Alauzeta" [skylark] because
> of a knight who loved her and called her "Rai" [ray]. And one day the
> knight came to the duchess and entered her bedroom. The woman,
> who saw him, then lifted up the hem of the coat as high as her neck
> and let herself fall onto the bed. And Bernart saw everything, since one
> of the lady's handmaids secretly showed it all to him. And it is for this
> *razo* that he composed the song that says: "Quan vei la lauzeta mover."

It suffices to glance at Bernart's song to realize that the author of
the *razo* (who claims to note family gossip, as Boccaccio will later
do for Dante's Beatrice) in fact does nothing other than bring the
troubadour's activity to its most extreme consequences. In the
apparent intention to relate the biographical anecdote that should
explain the poem, he completely invents it (and, to tell the truth,
invents it rather awkwardly) on the basis of the first three verses
of the poem ("Quan vei la lauzeta mover / de joi sos alas contra•l
rai / que s'oblid' es laissa chazer"). He thus constructs what is lived
on the basis of what is poeticized and not the inverse (as ought to
be done according to the biographical paradigm to which we moderns are accustomed).

It is not by chance that *vidas* and *razos* were written (as shown
by the Italianisms that proliferate in their lexis) in an Italian envi-

ronment or at the least for an Italian public. For it is precisely here, according to a canon that has its exemplary moments in the *Vita nuova* and the *Divine Comedy*, that life is conceived essentially as fable (*fabula*, that is, according to the etymological root, some- thing that essentially has to do with speech, with *fabulari*). What was, in the prologue to the Gospel of John, the inseparable dwelling of life in *logos* now becomes fable, comedy, life-in-speech (Ficino: "not life, but the fable of life"). It is good not to forget that in Romance literature, narrative (at least in the sense of short story) is born as the *razo* of lyric poetry. It is thanks to the poetic word's unspeakable dwelling *in the beginning* that something like lived ex- perience is made for the narrator. This is the "novella" that he lim- its himself to exemplifying.

VI

Adding an introduction to the second edition of his stories in 1956, Antonio Delfini wrote the longest *razo* for *Il ricordo della Basca* that any poet has ever composed for his work. In this case the *razo*, however, risks leading the reader astray, as had already happened in Provençal biographies. Delfini gestures in the direc- tion of the author's experience, but it is an experience (whether au- thentic or not) in no way exhausted in the biographical events that articulate it. And this is not because a future biographer will be un- able to verify that a fifteen-year-old Italian girl appeared in the street to the young artist on a summer day of a certain year, al- though it is already certain that he wrote *Poesie della fine del mondo* after having met a woman in Parma of whom it is all too easy to furnish an anagrammatic identity. The fact is that in Delfini, as in perhaps no other writer of the twentieth century, the indetermi- nateness of what is lived and what is poeticized is absolute, and *life is truly only what is made in speech.* In this sense, Delfini is the most authentic heir to the troubadour and Dolce Stil Novo tradition, and his entire work can be viewed as a singular draft, after seven centuries, on the culture that produced the Provençal biographies.

This is why when Delfini gave his love letters to Ugo and Michin

Guanda shortly before leaving for his last stay in Rome, he soberly made clear that he had given them not a "document of love" (as the recipients had mistakenly thought) but rather "an editorial offering." Here we find a correction of the "psychological mirror writing" that, according to a clever entry in Kafka's penultimate notebook, makes it seem that men are incessantly concerned to consolidate their life with *a posteriori* writings and justifications. With a decisive gesture Delfini shows, against every psychological reading, that "in reality man erects his life on his own justifications," since "here no one creates anything other than the possibility of spiritual life." It is, in any case, upon these archetypes that both Delfini and Kafka constructed their lives. Their biographical failure (or at least what appears as such in the inverted image of psychology) had to bear witness to—and not justify—the theological authenticity of writing (its dwelling in the *archē*).

VII

The worst way to misunderstand *Poesie della fine del mondo* would, however, be to read it as an immediate transcription of the life of Antonio Delfini (as "private revenge," as it has inappropriately been called). The note with which the collection ends leaves no doubt as to the position of these texts *in principio*, stating without ambiguity that "before the poet wrote there was not only no reality, but even the so-called reality of the public could not have been formulated." The claim of the antecedence of lived experience ("so-called real life") to the text belongs to "those who, not knowing how and not being able to live [that is, *in speech*], let nothing live, requiring that it be officially said that they live." (These are the sinister phantoms with obscene nicknames who so often appear in the text, where they have the same function as the *lauzengier*, the liar in Provençal songs.)

In Delfini, the world and life are born with speech and in speech. Why then does the title so clearly speak of the "end of the world" as something that has incontestably already happened (or that, in any case, is already happening)? How could it happen that speech is no longer capable of making life and maintaining it in its autonomy? And why does the speech of poetry here inaugurate not a *vita nova* but a cosmic and poetological catastrophe without precedent?

That Delfini was aware of the almost theological implications of this situation is implicit in one of the variant titles that figures among the author's notes: "God exists, but not the world." There could be no clearer way to express the drastic rupture of the life-poetry and *logos-cosmos* link that characterizes both the prologue to the Gospel of John and the dictation of the Dolce Stil Novo poets. In the other possible title preserved in Delfini's notes, "Scenes unleashed from life in the provinces," the adjective "unleashed" qualifies precisely life that has broken its tie to speech. This life, which is now simply "so-called real life," does not truly live; it can only "require" that it be said that it lives.

VIII

The catastrophe that is accomplished in these poems is therefore nothing less than the rupture of the poetic *razo*, the irreparable fragmentation of Delfini's dictation. But this laceration, which abandons life to its "true bad luck," immediately reverberates in poetry itself, which now becomes "bad poetry," poetry that the poet nevertheless cannot keep himself from writing ("it is my duty to write bad poetry," we read in the *incipit* of one the collection's key poems). The poet himself must thus—and this is the most atrocious event of the catastrophe—break his own dictation: "detach your horrible thought from pen / and from paper, this much is demanded and described here" (*distaccare il tuo orribile pensiero dalla penna / e dalla carta è quanto qui si vuole e si descrive*). This task is, in other words, exactly the opposite of the one Dante assigned to love poets through the figure of Bonagiunta in *Purgatorio* ("your pen follows close after who dictates" [*le vostre penne / di retro al dittator s'en vanno strette*]).[2] This is why the poet appears in the preface as a "murderer": he is condemned to kill his "lady," that is, his own life and his own poetry, his poetry-life ("the only way possible is death").

Hence the preliminary inversion of the feminine figure to which the love poets assigned the most integral image of their dictation. The woman (the "Basca," inscribed in the tradition of the Stilnovist and Provençal *senhal* among Beatrice, Giovanna, Miellz de Domna, Dezirada, Bon Vezi), who bore the unity of what is lived and what is poeticized and of life in speech, is now forcibly separated from writing and speech and transformed into bare life, the hideous and dark symbol "of fraud, betrayal, sin."

In a famous poem (whose verbal violence is in every way a match for Delfini's invectives), Arnaut Daniel evokes the figure of his own dictation as a woman (called Anya) whose body is broken in one area (in its *corn*, which philological rigor vainly attempts to identify as some feminine orifice or sphincter). In a kind of alchemical storm, all life threatens to escape from this area in the form of a viscous secretion, fetid smoke, and boiling refuse. In the lady of many names, in the "filthy, foul creature" or "infamous, dirty phantom," Delfini sees before him this life (the woman's life, hence also *his* life) in the act of definitively parting from speech and irreparably taking leave of poetry to become "real life." This separation, this unbearable reification, is the theme of Delfini's poems.

IX

It is therefore possible to understand why Delfini, in his preface, defines the *Poesie della fine del mondo* as an "anti-*Canzoniere*." Taken literally, this definition contains a precious reference not only to the literary tradition in which his collection is situated but also to the poetic experience that is accomplished in it.

In the *Vita nuova*, Dante consciously plays with the title of the work, so that it is impossible to decide once and for all if in the title one is to find a reference to what is lived or to what is poeticized, to the "book" (*libro*) of memory (in which one finds the title *Incipit vita nova*) or to the "booklet" (*libello*) in which the poet transcribes what the reader will read. The entry *Vita nova* thus delimits an undecidability between what is lived and what is poeticized. Consider instead the autograph title of Petrarch's *Canzoniere*:

Franceschi Petrarchae laureati poetae rerum vulgarium fragmenta (in the Chigi autograph, *fragmentorum liber*). Here the author, collecting poems in the collection that we are inappropriately accustomed to consider as the "organic adventure of a soul," distances them from lived experience with a decisive apotropaic gesture: it is merely a matter of "fragments in the vernacular." There could be no clearer way to say that the poetic universe that gave rise to the Provençal and Dolce Stil Novo projects had by now been left behind forever (the term *fragmenta*, which sounds so modern, must be restored its original sense as "splinters, shards," as in Isidore's *Etymologiae*, XX, 2, 18: *fragmenta, quia dividitur, ut fracta*). With a definitive movement away from the troubadour dictation, life now stands on one side, and poetry, on the other side, is only literature, mourning the irremediable death of Laura.

The *Poesie della fine del mondo* is an anti-*Canzoniere* because it is precisely this movement that Delfini refuses to accept at any price. Hence the furious war that the poet unleashes with his last forces against "reality," which is to the same degree a battle for poetry, a battle to keep the *Poesie della fine del mondo* from ever becoming a *Canzoniere*. This is why he fights against the "lady" of many heteronyms, the dark *senhal* of bare life and the luminous cipher of complete life: the girl with the flaming rose, the daughter, naturally, of Guido Cavalcanti (who here authoritatively represents the tradition of love poets).

Such is the apocalyptic vision (which, like every apocalypse, carries a historical index: one of the significant merits of the collection is to have captured the infernal *facies* of the 1950s at their end) that the *Poesie della fine del mondo* evokes and, at the same time, wards off with terrible scorn: a vision of life forever departing from speech (the avant-garde poetry of the 1960s was soon to register it actively in its own way) and presuming to state officially that it lives. *Delfini's* Poesie della fine del mondo *presents an experience that is perhaps unique in our century, the experience of a poet who cannot accept that his lived experience becomes biography, inexorably departs from speech, and becomes a real fact.*

This is why the most inhuman vision to which the poet bears

witness ("my courage was great!") is that the "lady" (his life) is observing him "even as [he] dies." Here, as in certain sudden breaks in the fabric of *Il ricordo della Basca,* what appears is an uncertain, febrile, and almost decayed image, the figure of an experience of poetic dictation that lies beyond the tradition of John and the Dolce Stil Novo as well as of Petrarch, a poetic dictation reserved for future poetic generations.

§ 6 Expropriated Manner

I

At the time of his death, on January 22, 1990, Giorgio Caproni was preparing a collection of poems whose title, thematic content, and relation to his previous work he had already announced, publicly or privately, on various occasions. Once he had finished the final draft of the poem he entitled "Res amissa" (shortly before January 2, 1987, if not on that very day),[1] Caproni noted the following on the manuscript:

> This poem will be the *subject* of my new book (if I succeed in writing it), followed by *variations*, just as in *Conte di K.* the subject is the Beast (evil) in its various forms and metamorphoses. We are all given something precious that we then lose irrevocably. (The Beast is Evil. The *res amissa* [the lost thing] is Good.)

Yet the first sketch of the poem (which, although not dated, is certainly from sometime after the first days of November 1986, the time of the visit to Cologne that furnished the occasion for the poet's reflections) already contained an annotation, first written in pencil and later nervously continued in pen. "We are all," it reads, "(without our remembering from whom) / given something precious / and we hide it away so carefully that we no longer remember where and, even, what the gift is Res amissa The opposite of the Count Center *loss*."

Later, Caproni explained in an interview with Domenico
Astengo:

> A little poem ["Generalizzando," "Generalizing"] that would, precisely
> to generalize, be something of a caption, or abbreviation, of a book
> that I am dreaming of, which, if I succeed in writing, I would call *Res
> amissa*. The idea came to me from a very banal fact that would take
> quite a while to explain here. It can happen to anyone that he hides
> away a precious thing so carefully as then to forget not only the thing's
> location, but also the actual nature of the object itself. This is a sub-
> ject that, for all its apparent simplicity, is very ambitious, especially so,
> I think, on account of the "variations" it can produce. This time what
> would be at stake would no longer be the hunt for the Beast, as in
> *Conte di Kevenhüller*, but rather the hunt for the lost Good. A Good
> left entirely *ad libitem* to the reader, a Good perhaps identifiable—for
> the believer—with Grace, given that there is such a thing as "admissi-
> ble Grace." With Grace or with anything else of the kind. (But I be-
> lieve the latter is not my case.)

For Caproni, the cue for such an "ambitious" variation may have
been even merely an entry in one of the reference books he rou-
tinely used, Palazzi's *Italian Dictionary*. This is suggested by an annotation made on one of the pages of the manuscript: "Palazzi Admissible (from the Latin *amittere*) that can be lost: admissible
grace." The speed with which this laconic *lemma* suffices to introduce one of the most arduous theological and ethical problems is
astonishing. (But whoever has held in his hands one of Caproni's
copies of the *Divine Comedy*, full of marginalia and worn out by
frequent use, will have no trouble imagining how much theology
he could transmit to his poetry.) The subject of the admissibility
of grace is, however, found for the first time precisely in an author
dear to Caproni, St. Augustine, who, in his *De natura et gratia*, dis-
cusses it in the context of his dispute with Pelagius.[2] The position
of Pelagius, one of the most impressive figures pushed to the margins of the Christian tradition by dogmatic orthodoxy, is well
known. The possibility of not sinning (*impeccantia*), Pelagius held,
inheres in human nature in an inseparable manner (and this leads
Augustine to coin the adjective *inamissibile*),[3] and there is there-

fore no need for the intervention of an ulterior grace, human nature being itself the immediate work of divine grace. With his usual
acumen, Augustine discerns the ultimate consequences of this doctrine and, afraid, retreats from them: the impossibility of distinguishing between human nature and a grace that has become inadmissible and, thus, the ruin of the very concept of sin. This is
why the Church consistently condemned Pelagianism and, against
all extremist currents, sustained the need both for the intervention
of grace and for its essentially "admissible" character, that is, its loss
through sin (Council of Trent, sess. 6, chap. 15: "If someone states
that once man has been justified, he can neither sin nor lose
Grace . . . anathema").

Caproni's idea is a kind of extreme Pelagianism: grace is a gift so
profoundly infused in human nature that it cannot be made
known to it, being always already a *res amissa* and always already
unappropriable. Inadmissible, since it is always already lost, and
lost on account of being—like life and nature itself—too inti-
mately possessed, too "carefully (irrecoverably) hidden away." This
is why Caproni, explaining to Domenico Astengo the sense of the
"thorn of nostalgia" (*spina della nostalgia*) in the poem "Generalizzando," specified that "the content or object of such nostalgia is
nostalgia itself." Here the good that is given is not, in fact, something that was once known and then forgotten (the "then" [*poi*] of
"Generalizzando" is not chronological but purely logical). The gift
that is received is, instead, forever lost from the beginning. The
anaphoric "it" (*ne*) that opens *Res amissa* ("I find no trace of it"
[*Non ne trovo traccia*]) remains forever deprived of the anaphorized
term that alone could furnish it with its denotative value.

With a characteristic gesture, Caproni, drastically identifying
grace and nature in the figure of the *res amissa*, renders obsolete the
categorial distinctions on which Western theology and ethics are
founded—or rather, he complicates them and displaces them into
a region in which their sense radically changes. One could, that is,
repeat for Caproni the *boutade* with which Walter Benjamin defined his own relation to theology when he compared it to that between an ink pad and ink: the ink pad is, to be sure, full of ink,

but if it were up to the pad, not even a drop of ink would remain. This is why the term "negative theology" (whose misuse the poet himself avoided) is neither useful nor adequate. One ought, instead, to note how in Caproni, the tradition of modern atheological poetry (Caproni also calls it "pathotheology") reaches its extreme outcome, even its collapse. In this tradition (if one may speak of a tradition), Caproni's poetry represents something like Astápovo, the small train station where Tolstoy died: a casual stopping point from which it is impossible to turn back, on a trip leading nowhere and, at the same time, in flight beyond every familiar figure of the human and the divine.

II

A date of birth can be assigned, with reasonable accuracy, to poetic atheology: it is the day on which Hölderlin, at the dawn of the nineteenth century, corrected the last two verses of the poem "Dichterberuf" ("The Poet's Calling"). Where the first version read:

> Und keiner Würde brauchts, und keiner
> Waffen, solange der Gott nicht fehlet
>
> (And there is no need for worth and for
> arms, as long as the god is not absent)

Hölderlin corrects:

> Und keiner Waffen brauchts, und keiner
> Listen, so lange, bis Gottes Fehl hilft.
>
> (And there is no need for arms and for
> cunning, as long as God's absence aids.)[4]

What begins here (without being consigned to any tradition in the strict sense, but instead rebounding, so to speak, from poet to poet) is not a new theology; and it is not even a negative theology (which posits pure Being in withdrawing from it every real predicate and essence). Nor is it an atheistic Christology (as in a certain contemporary social theology). Hölderlin's correction marks the point at which the divine and the human alike are ruined, at which poetry opens onto a region that is uncertain and devoid of a subject, flattened on the transcendental, and which can be defined only by the Hölderlinian euphemism, "betrayal of the sacred." ("Thus," we read in the *Notes* to Hölderlin's translation of Sophocles' *Oedipus*, "man forgets himself and the god turns away, but sacredly, as a traitor. At the extreme limit of suffering nothing remains but the conditions of space and time.") What characterizes poetic atheology as opposed to every negative theology is its singular coincidence of nihilism and poetic practice, thanks to which poetry becomes the laboratory in which all known figures are undone and new, parahuman or semidivine creatures emerge: Hölderlin's half-god, Kleist's marionette, Nietzsche's Dionysus, the angel and the doll in Rilke, Kafka's Odradek as well as Celan's "Medusa-head" and "automaton" and Montale's "pearly snail's trace." (In this sense, atheology had already begun when Provençal and Dolce Stil Novo lyric poetry transformed poetry into the chamber or *stanza* in which an absolute experience of desubjectivization and deindividuation went hand in hand with the ceremonious invention of figures of delirium: the woman-angel and the love-spirits of the Dolce Stil Novo poets and the partial bodies of the troubadours, all under the sign of the paradoxical identification of poetry with the female body.)

In Caproni, all figures of atheology reach a point at which they take leave. "Discharge" or "taking leave" [*congedo*] is truly the exemplary moment of the later Caproni (I take the later Caproni to begin with the publication of *Congedo del viaggiatore cerimonioso* in 1965). But whereas Hölderlin's infidelity held fast precisely to the hope that "the memory of the heavenly ones might not end," here what asserts itself is the "decision to make do without," in which even atheological pathos is definitively set aside, the memory of gods and men eclipsed and a way cleared to a landscape that is now entirely empty of figures. This is why Caproni, perhaps more than any other contemporary poet, succeeded in expressing without any shadow of nostalgia or nihilism the *ethos* and almost the *Stimmung* of the "solitude without God" of which he speaks in *Franco cac-*

ciatore's "Inserto." ("Basically unbreathable. Hard and colorless like quartz. Black and transparent [and cutting] like obsidian. The happiness that it can give is unspeakable. It's the entry—every hope neatly cut off—to every possible freedom. Including that [the serpent that bites its tail] of believing in God, while knowing—definitely—that there is no God and that he doesn't exist.")[5] But the infinite "ceremony" of taking leave, which had already been accomplished in *Franco cacciatore* and in *Conte* (and it is then truly possible, as has been observed,[6] to read in "Rifiuto dell'Invitato" something like a Last Supper that has become entirely immemorable), is now replaced by taking leave from leave-taking itself, to penetrate into regions of ever greater expropriation between man and God.

In this sense, it is decisive that both *Conte* and *Res amissa* have at their center a figure of impropriety. The Beast of *Conte* is, in fact, something that as such belongs to no one (the *fera bestia* is, in juridical terms, the very type of the *res nullius*). And the good that is at issue in the last collection is a *res amissa*, not in the sense of a *res derelicta* (which, according to Roman jurists, becomes an object of property once again as soon as someone takes hold of it), but as something that can never be appropriated. The Beast of *Conte* was, after all, an allegory not so much of evil (one could equally well, according to an equivocation typical of Caproni, discern in it a cipher of life and language) as of evil's radical impropriety, such that the only true evil was nothing other than the stubborn and useless human attempt to capture evil and make it one's own. The *res amissa* is, in the same way, nothing but the unappropriability and unfigurability of the good (whether this good is conceived, in turn, as nature or grace, life or language—or, as one reads in the first draft of the poem, freedom). The Beast and the *res amissa* are therefore not two things but instead two faces of the same expropriation of a single gift. Or rather, the *res amissa* is nothing other than the Beast become definitively unappropriable, the discharge from every hunt and every will to appropriation (according to an indication that is also common to the late Betocchi: "Evil and good are two mirrors / of the same illusion: that is / to live master of one's own being").[7] This is how one must understand the tight correspondence suggested by Caproni between the two collections: together they constitute the panels of a diptych bearing the introduction to a new ethos, that is, to the new dwelling of the "disinhabitants" of the earth.

III

Why does poetry matter to us? The ways in which answers to this question are offered testify to its absolute importance. For the field of possible respondents is clearly divided between those who affirm the significance of poetry only on condition of altogether confusing it with life and those for whom the significance of poetry is instead exclusively a function of its isolation from life. Both groups thereby betray their apparent intention: the first, because they sacrifice poetry to the life into which they resolve it; the second, because in the last analysis they are convinced of poetry's impotence with respect to life. Romanticism and aestheticism, which confuse life and poetry at every step, are just as foolish as Olympian classicism and well-meaning secularism, which everywhere keep life and poetry apart, destining humanity to transmit a patrimony that is holy but that has become useless precisely in the issue that should have become decisive.

Opposed to these two positions is the experience of the poet, who affirms that if poetry and life remain infinitely divergent on the level of the biography and psychology of the individual, they nevertheless become absolutely indistinct at the point of their reciprocal desubjectivization. And—at that point—they are united not immediately but in a medium. This medium is language. The poet is he who, in the word, produces life. Life, which the poet produces in the poem, withdraws from both the lived experience of the psychosomatic individual and the biological unsayability of the species.

At the origins of Italian poetry, in the terzina in which Dante defines the Dolce Stil Novo, this unity of lived experience and what is poeticized [*il poetato*] in the medium of language at a point that is both singular and without a subject was presented as the proper task of the poet:

> Ed io a lui: I' mi son un che, quando
> Amor mi spira, noto, e a quel modo
> ch'è ditta dentro vo significando.

> (And I to him, "I am one who, when
> Love inspires me, takes note, and
> goes setting it forth after the fashion
> which he dictates within me.")[8]

Here the "I" of the poet is from the beginning desubjectivized into a generic *un* ("one"), and it is this *un* (something more—or less—than the "exemplary universal" of which Caproni speaks) that, in the dictation of love, experiences the indissoluble unity of lived experience and what is poeticized. The unity of poetry and life does not have a metaphorical character at this level. On the contrary, poetry matters because the individual who experiences this unity in the medium of language undergoes an anthropological change that is, in the context of the individual's natural history, every bit as decisive as was, for the primate, the liberation of the hand in the erect position or, for the reptile, the transformation of limbs that changed it into a bird.

Take the legendary cycle of *Versi livornesi* for Annina Picchi in Caproni's *Il seme del piangere*. Whoever is not wholly insensitive to the problems and tradition of poetry will remain astonished at this striking resurgence of the Sicilian *canzonetta* and Cavalcanti's *ballata* in the celebration of the "splendid invention" (Mengaldo) of an amorous relation with a mother-maiden. One cannot, however, grasp the poetic task that is fulfilled here as long as one considers this poetry in the context of the psychological and biographical question of the incestuous sublimation of the mother-son relationship—which is to say, as long as one does not recognize the anthropological change that takes place in these verses. For here there are neither figures of memory nor even *amor de lonh*. Rather, love, in a kind of temporal (and hence not merely spatial, as in the Dolce Stil Novo poets) shamanism, encounters *for the first time* its love object in another time. This is why there can be no trace of incest: the mother is truly a girl, "*a* cyclist," and the "betrothed" poet literally loves her *at first sight.* In this sense, Caproni's man belongs to a different *phylon* from the man of Oedipus: leaping in one bound over the lugubrious chronological order of the family, the edict of *Versi livornesi* announces the end of Oedipus and the incestuous family. Whoever continues, when confronted with this poetry, to speak in terms of incest and psychology cannot but play the part of the exemplary critic who, with nowhere to go, lingers over the dead railway track of poetic anthropology. Hence the terrible reuniting of the two figures *ad portam inferi,* when the girl ends by confusing herself with the oedipal mother and searches in vain for the keys and the ring she cannot have. The infernal threshold here does not so much mark the passage from the reign of the living to that of the dead as it marks the point of fusion, in the living furnace of poetic fantasy, at which the two pass through each other. The death of Annina Picchi, exactly like that of Beatrice, is not the death of an individual but the tremendous collision between two irreconcilable worlds.

These are therefore not "family poems"[9] but rather, as in the poem to the son Attilio Mauro in *Muro della terra,* temporal inversions and phylogenetic exchanges in which family hierarchies become unrecognizable. Caproni, in other words, succeeds where Pascoli perhaps tried, but failed—to confuse and erotically transfigure the walls of the *domus* and the *family,* in order ultimately to encounter creatures who, wholly reborn to themselves and to others, once lived there. This is why it is not senseless to compare the girl of *Versi livornesi* with Pascoli's "La tessitrice." Just as Cavalcanti and the Dolce Stil Novo poets (on the epochal threshold of an anthropological change that would for the first time dislocate sexuality beyond the confines of reproduction of the species) had, through their "spirits" or *spiritelli,* presented in a living figure the separate Sicilian image of the woman painted in the mind, so the mute pantomime of memory that imprisons Pascoli's "virgin" is dissolved, in Caproni, in the cheerful gesture of the embroideress and the lively, noisy run of the cyclist. The transformation of the

oedipal family that failed in Pascoli's San Mauro is happily accomplished in Livorno in Caproni's experiment, in which the valence
of "progressive anthropology," which Schlegel and the Jena Ro-
mantics assigned to poetry, shows its full truth. (By a singular coincidence that we record here only out of the love of curiosity,
Caproni is also the name of the physician who, in Barga, treated
the dying Pascoli.)

IV

Anthropological changes correspond, in language, to poetological changes. These are all the more difficult to register in that they
do not simply represent stylistic or rhetorical progressions, but
rather call into question the very borders between languages. The
linguist Ernst Lewy, who was Benjamin's professor in Berlin, in 1913
published a brief monograph entitled *Zur Sprache des alten Goethes,
Ein Versuch über die Sprache des Einzelnen* (*On the Language of the
Old Goethe: An Essay on the Language of the Individual*). Like many
before him, Lewy had noted the transformation of Goethe's language in his late works. But whereas critics had accounted for this
transformation in terms of senile stylistic devices, Lewy, who was
an expert glottologist and a specialist in Ural-Altaic languages, observed that in the old Goethe German evolved from the characteristic morphology of Indo-European languages toward forms characteristic of agglutinative languages, such as Turkish. Among these
changes, Lewy listed (1) the tendency toward extremely unusual
composed adjectives; (2) the prevalence of the nominal sentence;
and (3) the progressive disappearance of the article.

We know of only one other example of this type of analysis con-
ducted on the work of a writer: Contini's "brief guide" to Pizzuto's
Paginette.[10] Contini discerns in Pizzuto's stubborn elision of the
verb, in "his kind of ablative absolutes," in his dislocated or alter-
native agreements (more imaginable in a language with cases) a
tendency not only toward archaic Indo-European and its nominal
style but also "beyond the borders recognized in Indo-European,"
toward monosyllabic languages (such as Chinese, for example).

It is not surprising that Lewy's essay elicited Benjamin's enthusiasm. For here the language of the individual becomes the site of a dislocation and experimental change in which what comes to light is the very "pure language" (Dante spoke, in a sense that is not so dissimilar, of an "illustrious vernacular" [*volgare illustre*]) that, according to Benjamin, stands between languages without coinciding with any of them (and whose proper place he found in translation).

Tensions and extremisms of this kind, which are not uncommon in the work of old artists (it is enough, for painting, to think of Titian or the late Michelangelo), are usually classified by critics as mannerisms. The Alexandrian grammarians observed early on that Plato's style, which is so limpid in the youthful dialogues, becomes difficult, affected, and overly paratactic in the late dialogues. Similar remarks (except that here one usually speaks of madness and not senility) have been and can be made concerning Hölderlin's writings after the translations of Sophocles, which are so divided between the harsh technique of the hymns and the frozen sweetness of the poems signed with the heteronym Scardinelli. Analogously, in Melville's last novels (think of *Pierre, or the Ambiguities* or *The Confidence-Man*) mannerisms and digressions proliferate to the point of breaking the very form of the novel, carrying it away toward other, less legible genres (the philosophical treatise or the erudite notebook).

Terms of "manner" are certainly apt, to the extent that they register the phenomenon's irreducibility to a procedure of stylistic evolution. Here, however, it will be necessary to overthrow or abandon the usual hierarchical relation between style and manner, and to consider their connection in a new light. These concepts designate two realities that are correlates, yet irreducible to each other. If style marks the artist's most characteristic trait, manner registers an inverse process of expropriation and exclusion. It is as if the old poet, who found his style and reached perfection in it, now forgets it in order to advance the singular claim of expressing himself solely through impropriety. In the areas in which it has been most rigorously defined (art history and psychiatry), manner in fact designates a polar process: manner is an exaggerated adhesion to a usage or model (stereotype, or repetition) and, at the same time, a show of absolute excess with relation to it (extravagance, or singularity). In art history, mannerism thus "presupposes the knowledge of a style to which one believes oneself to adhere, but which one instead unconsciously seeks to avoid" (Pinder). For psychiatrists, on the other hand, the mode of being of the mannerist consists in showing "impropriety in the sense of not being oneself" and, at the same time, the will to earn thereby one's own terrain and status (Binswanger). Analogous observations could be made with respect to the writer and his language; and it ought not to be forgotten that a significant current of Italian literature (Gadda is exemplary here) is characterized by nothing other than taking its distance, so to speak, from language through an excessive, mannered adhesion to it (as if the writer excluded himself from the language in which he wrote in order to be overcome by it).

Only in their reciprocal relation do style and manner acquire their true sense beyond the proper and the improper. The free gesture of the writer lives in the tension between these two poles: style is an *expropriating appropriation*, a sublime negligence, a self-forgetting in the proper; manner is an *appropriating expropriation*, a presentiment or remembrance of oneself in the improper. Not only in the old poet but in every great writer (Shakespeare!) there is a manner that distances itself from style, a style that expropriates itself into manner. At its height, writing even consists in precisely the interval—or, rather, the passage—between the two. Perhaps in every field but most of all in language, use is a polar gesture: on the one hand, appropriation and habit; on the other, expropriation and nonidentity. And "usage" (in its whole semantic field, as both "to use" and "to be used to") is the perpetual oscillation between a homeland and an exile—dwelling.

v

In twentieth-century Italian literature, Caproni's late poetry constitutes perhaps the most exemplary testimony to this divergence. Here one finds, first of all, at least two of the traits noted by Lewy and Contini: the tendency to anomalous adjectival compounds (to take only *Res amissa*: "biancoflauta," "flautoscomparsa") and a nominal style (the extreme case is "Invenzioni," in which seven out of eight sentences have no verb). Pasolini's joking remark (which the poet himself liked to repeat) that Caproni speaks not Italian but "Capronian" is in this sense justified. But what is essential is that this transgressive manner exerts itself on the element that, more than any other, characterizes poetry: meter. For at a certain point the poet who had reached excellence both in the harsh, almost stony technique of *Passaggio d'Enea* and in the sweet technique[11] of *Il seme del piangere* sets aside his song and—repeating on a different plane the gesture with which the youthful orchestra player, called upon one evening to play first violin, smashed the wood of his violin—now undoes and breaks up his precious poetic instrument. Taking up an expression of Dante's, Caproni gives the name "musical tie" (*legame musaico*) to the formal relation that is here dissolved—or rather, suspended. In the interview with Astengo, the relevant passage in Dante's *Convivio* ("nothing harmonized through the musical tie can be transferred from its own phrasing into that of another without ruining its sweetness and harmony" [*nulla cosa per legame musaico armonizzata si può de la sua loquela in altra transmutare senza rompere tutta sua dolcezza e armonia*]) is cited concerning the impossibility of translation. And translation (in particular that of Céline, from whom Caproni may have borrowed his use of ellipsis dots; but also, in an opposite direction, that of Wilhelm Busch) is the laboratory in which Caproni prepared for the "transformation" that marked his late poetry, that is, its progressive expropriation of the "musical tie."

(Might the reader allow a digression. More than any other European national literature, twentieth-century Italian poetry kept itself most faithful to the need for metrical closure in poetic discourse. German lyric poetry has been familiar with *freie Rhythmen* [those, for example, of Novalis's *Hymns to the Night* and Rilke's *Duino Elegies*] for over a century; and French poetry definitively turns its back on the metrical tradition with Mallarmé's "Un coup de dés." In Italy, on the other hand, the twentieth century [despite

d'Annunzio's free verse—but on this see Lucini's observations!]
marks one of the peaks of musical versification, one without counterpart in other European languages. Hence its untranslatability.
Rilke, for all the profundity of the content of his poems, often remains the prisoner of a soft musicality as far as rhythm is concerned, justifying Benjamin's characterization of him as the poet of
Jugendstil. Pascoli, whose poems' subjects are often downright in-
sipid, is without rival in Europe in his mastery of the musical tie.
This is why Pintor's translation of *Neue Gedichte* in *Poemi convivi-
ali* is equal, if not superior, to the original, while a translation not
only of Pascoli but even of Penna or Caproni will never succeed in
giving the vaguest idea of the original.)

It has already been noted how this progressive transfiguration of
the musical tie articulates itself in Caproni's last collections. The
traditional measure of the verse is drastically contracted, and the
three ellipsis dots (which Caproni himself compares to the *pizzi-
cato* that functions to break up the development of the melodic
phrase in Schubert's op. 63 quartet) mark the impossibility of com-
pleting the prosodic theme. The verse is thus reduced to its limit-
ing elements: enjambment (if it is true that enjambment is the only
criterion that allows one to distinguish poetry from prose) and
caesura (which Hölderlin defined as "antirhythmic" and which ex-
pands to the point of devouring the whole rhythm).[12]

One ought to speak, therefore, neither of free nor of typograph-
ically fragmented verse, but rather of aprosody (in the sense in
which neurologists, who speak of aphasia when characterizing dis-
turbances to the logico-discursive aspect of language, define aprosody as the alteration of language's tonal and rhythmic aspects). And
one ought to recognize that this aprosody is, as is obvious, patiently
calculated and obsessively ordered (Caproni's publishers were familiar with the poet's almost maniacal attention to the typograph-
ical arrangement), which makes it no less destructive.

According to the polar character of poetic writing that has already been noted, however, this estrangement from the prosodic element produces an opposite effect: the mock verse of the counter-
Caproni.[13] One may wonder where the invasive proliferation of

this (metrically trivial) humming comes from, accompanying the broken song of the last poems almost like whistling in the middle of the severest hymn, giving consistency to the paradox of a poet who lives in personal union with a counter-poet. These little verses are the splinters chipped off from the implacable work of expropriation that characterizes Caproni's supreme manner.

In this sense, *Res amissa* truly contains the final sense of its poetry. For now poetry itself has, for the old poet, become the *res amissa* in which it is impossible to distinguish between nature and grace, dwelling and gift, possession and expropriation. Hovering, poised in a kind of transcendental mimicry between the aprosody of interrupted song and overly harmonious little verses, poetry now reaches a domain forever beyond the proper and the improper, salvation and ruin. This is the unappropriable legacy that Caproni's expropriated manner leaves to Italian poetry, and that no benefit of inventory will permit it to elude. Like an animal whose mutation has carried it so far outside its species that we can neither assign it to another *phylon* nor know if it will pass its mutation on to others, poetry—now both unrecognizable and all too familiar—has definitively become a *res amissa* for us. This is why it is impossible to say whether even one of all the poetry books that are being published and that will certainly continue to be published will be at the level of the event that has happened here. We can only say that here something ends forever and something begins, and that what begins begins only in what ends.

§ 7 The Celebration of the Hidden Treasure

I own the copy of Spinoza's *Ethics* that belonged to Elsa Morante; it was given to me by Carlo Cecchi in remembrance of Elsa. It is the edition published in Sansoni's "Classici della filosofia" series in 1963, and it reproduces the Latin text and notes of Giovanni Gentile's 1915 Laterza edition, adding to it an Italian translation by Gaetano Durante. Elsa's special veneration for Spinoza is illustrated, as you know, by his location at the top of the mock genealogical tree in her "Canzone degli F.P. e degli I.M." ("*Canzone* of the Happy Few and the Unhappy Many") alongside Simone Weil, Giordano Bruno, Gramsci, Rimbaud, Mozart, Joan of Arc, Giovanni Bellini, Plato, and Rembrandt. As I write this list, I notice that the philosophers are in the majority. This might be a point of departure for an investigation of Elsa's relation to philosophy, which is anything but settled; but this is not the project I wish to pursue.

It is not surprising, then, that the copy of the *Ethics* in question contains various marginal comments in Elsa's handwriting, in the form of stars, lines, question marks, exclamation points, and, finally—in one significant place—a genuine annotation. I would like to speak to you briefly about this last marginal comment, since it bears witness to a sharp and continuous disagreement that, I think, particularly illuminates Elsa's tenacious philosophical convictions.

But first let us take a look at the markings that precede this one. The first, in the shape of a pretty red star, accompanies the definitions that open the first book of the *Ethics*, in particular the sixth, that is, the famous definition of God: "By God I mean an absolutely infinite being; that is, substance consisting of infinite attributes, each of which expresses eternal and infinite essence."[1] Elsa marked the explication that immediately follows: "I say 'absolutely infinite,' not 'infinite in kind.' For if a thing is only infinite in its kind, one may deny that it has infinite attributes. But if a thing is absolutely infinite, whatever expresses essence and does not involve any negation belongs to its essence."[2]

A few pages later, a double red line appears in the margin of the scholium to proposition 10, where one reads: "Now if anyone asks by what mark we can distinguish between different substances, let him read the following Propositions, which show that in Nature there exists only one substance, absolutely infinite."[3]

It is easy to sense how Elsa could have been attracted to Spinoza's idea of the unity of divine substance constituted by an infinity of attributes, each of which expresses an eternal and infinite essence. And it is certainly not surprising to see another red star marking the important corollary to proposition 25, which reads: "Particular things are nothing but affections of the attributes of God; that is, modes wherein the attributes of God find expression in a definite and determinate way."[4] That all things and all living beings are nothing but the modes in which the divine attributes explicate and express themselves—here is another idea that must have been particularly congenial to Elsa and that even constituted one of her deepest convictions.

After this point, the markings become rarer and rarer, until they disappear altogether in Part Three, precisely the part that, with its treatment of the passions, must have immensely interested Elsa. The annotations start up again suddenly in the scholium to proposition 37 of Part Four, where a double series of alternating question marks and exclamation points mark both the Latin text and the translation. They introduce the following sharp, discordant observation in the bottom margin of the book: "Oh Baruch! I feel very sorry for you, but here you did not UNDERSTAND." The passage from which these words distance themselves reads as follows:

From this it is clear that the requirement to refrain from slaughtering beasts is founded on groundless superstition and womanish compassion rather than on sound reason. The principle of seeking our own advantage teaches us to be in close relationship with men, not with beasts or things whose nature is different from human nature, and that we have the same right over them as they over us. Indeed, since every individual's right is defined by his virtue or power, man's right over beasts is far greater than their rights over man. I do not deny that beasts feel; I am denying that we are on that account debarred from paying heed to our own advantage and from making use of them as we please and dealing with them as best suits us, seeing that they do not agree with us in nature and their emotions are different in nature from human emotions.[5]

The reasons for Elsa's disagreement seem all too obvious. Moreover, Spinoza's thesis is in some way an affront to our sensibility, and it brings to mind an episode in the biography of the philosopher that has often been contrasted with his image: "He looked," Colerus writes, "for spiders, which he would then force to fight against one another, or else for flies, which he would cast into the spider's web; and he observed these battles with so much pleasure that he often burst out laughing."

I must pause on this point, but neither to clarify a problem in the interpretation of Spinoza nor to defend the coherence of the philosopher. Rather, I wish to cast some light on the reasons for his disagreement with Elsa, which may in fact be less obvious than appears at first sight.

At the end of the passage that I just cited, Spinoza refers to the scholium of proposition 57 of Part Three. "Hence it follows," Spinoza writes,

that the emotions of animals that are called irrational (for now that we know the origin of mind we can by no means doubt that beasts have feelings) differ from the emotions of men as much as their nature differs from human nature. Horse and man are indeed carried away by lust to procreate, but the former by equine lust, the latter by human lust. So too the lusts and appetites of insects, fishes and birds are bound to be of various different kinds. So although each individual lives content with the nature wherewith he is endowed and rejoices in it, that life wherewith each is content and that joy are nothing other than the idea of soul (anima) of the said individual, and so the joy of the one differs from the joy of the other as much as the essence of the one differs from the essence of the other.[6]

The fact is that for Spinoza, all living beings without distinction express God's attributes in a certain determinate manner. But this absolute ontological proximity, not only between men and animals but also between all individuals of every species, is confirmed by their divergence on the plane of ethics. Precisely because they are all modes of a single substance, they can gather together or not gather together according to the diversity of their natures. The great right of man over animals does not, therefore, express a hierarchical or ontological supremacy; instead it corresponds to the general diversity of living beings. If, for the sake of hypothesis, there were a man whose existence was increased by the spider or the fly, or who could develop friendships with them, this man according to Spinoza would do well to take greatest care to protect these creatures' lives.

If we turn now to Elsa and more closely consider her ideas on animals and the reasons for her disagreement with Spinoza, we may be in for a surprise. What, for Elsa, is the reason for the special dignity of the animal, which Spinoza did not "understand"? It is simple: animals are the sole witnesses to the existence of earthly paradise and, therefore, the sole proof of man's lost Edenic state. This absolutely serious thesis is jokingly stated in the two fragments of 1950 entitled "Paradiso terrestre" and "Vero re degli animali," where Elsa speaks "of the extreme proof of mercy that the Eternal Father, despite His severity, gave to man, leaving him the company of animals, who had not eaten from the tree of knowledge as he had." But this conviction is present to a certain extent in all her works. In his notebooks, Kafka (the only writer whom Elsa confessed to have been influenced by) says that "there were three different ways to punish original sin: the mildest kind was immediately inflicted, and it was the banishment from paradise; the second was the destruction of paradise itself; and the third—and this is said to have been the worst punishment of all—was the barring of access to the eternal way, with everything else left as before." Elsa begins by accepting the first possibility: man has obtained the knowledge of good and evil and has, therefore, been banished from Eden; animals, immune to this shadow, have remained in the Garden. But the animals' negative privilege marks them off from man by an unbridgeable abyss, dividing men and animals far more than the diversity of natures separated them in Spinoza. The wound that traverses Elsa's work is not simply, as in Spinoza, the divergence between forms of life, the discordant plurality of the different modes of expressing a single substance. It is instead a fracture that passes through the inside of life itself, dividing it like the sharpest blade according to whether or not it remained in Eden and whether or not it was contaminated by the shadow of knowledge. Pure animal life (which is clearly also present in the natural life of man) and human life, Edenic existence and the knowledge of good and evil, nature and language: these are the edges of the wound that the Judeo-Christian inheritance marked in Elsa's thought, and that separate her from her beloved cats far more than Spinoza was divided from his spiders and other so-called "irrational beasts."

Yet if this is true, if what Baruch did not understand is this irreparable fracture, how can it then be that the philosopher's name figures (by virtue of a choice which the manuscripts show to have been meditated) at the summit of the genealogical tree in *Canzone*, under the title "the celebration of the hidden treasure"? I have often asked myself what the meaning of this singular formula could be. What celebration is at issue here? And what is its hidden treasure? And how did Elsa come to be reconciled with Baruch?

A hint of a possible answer is contained in Elsa's discussion of the relation between light and bodies in her text on Beato Angelico. "Colors," Elsa writes, "are a gift of light, which makes use of bodies . . . to transform its invisible celebration into an epiphany. . . . It is well known that to the eyes of *idiots* (poor and rich alike) the hierarchy of splendors culminates in the sign of gold. For those who do not know the true, inner alchemy of light, earthly mines are the place of a hidden treasure." The "celebration of the hidden treasure" is therefore the becoming visible, in bodies, of the alchemy of light. This alchemy is both a spiritualization of matter and a materialization of light. And it is this "celebration" that the knowledge of the third kind revealed to Spinoza *sub quadam aeternitatis specie.*

The late encounter with Beato Angelico thus coincides with a "Spinozist" moment in which Elsa sets aside her tragic "prejudices" and Edenic mythology to approach her supreme vision, which—like comprehension in Spinoza—is far more despairing than every tragedy and far more festive than every comedy. Here the reconciliation with Spinoza is important, for it acts as a counterbalance to a temptation in Elsa that was certainly strong. All greatness contains an inner threat with which it is in constant combat and to which it at times succumbs. And every comprehension of a work that does not keep in mind this part of the shadow (which is absolutely not of the psychological order) risks falling into hagiography. For Elsa, this shadowy part coincides with the tragico-sacrificial mythology that identifies the creature's bare life as the most absolute innocence and as the most extreme guilt, as sanctity and as malediction, and as darkness and as light. This mythology takes these two aspects to be indistinguishable, according to the ambiguous meaning (which is wrongly thought to be original) of the adjective *sacer.* It is a conception of this kind that leads Simone Weil, in her *Cahiers,* to evoke the figure of the scapegoat, in whom sacrificial innocence and guilt, sanctity and abjection, victim and executioner are founded for the sake of catharsis. It is necessary to recognize this temptation in both Morante and Weil for what it is, and to search in their own work for the antidotes contained there when they refuse the temptation of the spirit of the desert.

For Elsa, this is the moment at which she abandons the first and the third of Kafka's hypotheses for the sake of the second—that of the irreparable and retroactive destruction of paradise. And it coincides with the turn marked by the second half of the 1960s (in particular by 1968, thanks to a kind of ironic historical cipher), which Cesare Garboli has powerfully reconstructed in psychological terms and which I would like to attempt to understand from a philosophical perspective.

In the collection of aphorisms that Kafka composed in Zurau between 1917 and 1918 and that Max Brod pompously entitled *Observations on Sin, Pain, Hope and the True Way*, we find the following singular statement, which seems to me to contain the epitome of the shift at issue: "The fact that only the spiritual world exists deprives us of hope and gives us certainty."

In *Nine Doors*, Jírí Langer holds that this is "the most beautiful Hassidic doctrine":

> The most beautiful Hassidic teaching is without doubt the doctrine of the spirituality of matter. According to this doctrine, all of matter is full of the spiritual sparks of divine holiness. The purely physical expressions of human life—like eating and drinking, washing and sleeping, dancing and the act of love—are dematerialized by Hassidism and transformed into nobler religious exercises.

It is likely that Elsa knew this text. But, from the Kafkaesque perspective that she fully shared, this beautiful certainty is also what deprives us of hope. The loss of hope (even of that retrospective hope, nostalgia for Eden) is the terrible price that the mind must pay when it reaches the incandescent point of certainty. This is why Spinoza's celebration is the "celebration of the hidden treasure." The treasure is hidden not because someone or something buried or covered it over but because it is now exposed, beyond both tragedy and comedy in the absolute and despairing absence of all secrets. The knowledge of good and evil, which had so deeply marked Morante's tales with its shadow, finally shows itself to be, in Spinoza's sober words, nothing but the knowledge of sadness and delight; it is now up to the "angelic wild beasts" and the "ferocious knights," to men and to animals. The definitive taking leave of the lost Eden is, in this sense, the bitterest and most difficult point in Elsa's creative adventure. It is the essential moment inscribed by her "Addio," in the "blue nights without redemption," on the very threshold of *Il mondo salvato dai ragazzini*.

§ 8 The End of the Poem

My plan, as you can see summarized before you in the title of this lecture, is to define a poetic institution that has until now remained unidentified: the end of the poem.

To do this, I will have to begin with a claim that, without being trivial, strikes me as obvious—namely, that poetry lives only in the tension and difference (and hence also in the virtual interference) between sound and sense, between the semiotic sphere and the semantic sphere. This means that I will attempt to develop in some technical aspects Valéry's definition of poetry, which Jakobson considers in his essays in poetics: "The poem: a prolonged hesitation between sound and sense" (*Le poème, hésitation prolongée entre le son et le sens*). What is a hesitation, if one removes it altogether from the psychological dimension?

Awareness of the importance of the opposition between metrical segmentation and semantic segmentation has led some scholars to state the thesis (which I share) according to which the possibility of enjambment constitutes the only criterion for distinguishing poetry from prose. For what is enjambment, if not the opposition of a metrical limit to a syntactical limit, of a prosodic pause to a semantic pause? "Poetry" will then be the name given to the discourse in which this opposition is, at least virtually, possible; "prose" will be the name for the discourse in which this opposition cannot take place.

Medieval authors seem to have been perfectly conscious of the eminent status of this opposition, even if it was not until Nicolò Tibino (in the fourteenth century) that the following perspicuous definition of enjambment was formulated: "It often happens that the rhyme ends, without the meaning of the sentence having been completed" (*Multiocens enim accidit quod, finita consonantia, adhuc sensus orationis non est finitus*).

All poetic institutions participate in this noncoincidence, this schism of sound and sense—rhyme no less than caesura. For what is rhyme if not a disjunction between a semiotic event (the repetition of a sound) and a semantic event, a disjunction that brings the mind to expect a meaningful analogy where it can find only homophony?

Verse is the being that dwells in this schism; it is a being made of *murs et paliz*, as Brunetto Latini wrote, or an *être de suspens*, in Mallarmé's phrase. And the poem is an organism grounded in the perception of the limits and endings that define—without ever fully coinciding with, and almost in intermittent dispute with—sonorous (or graphic) units and semantic units.

Dante is fully conscious of this when, at the moment of defining the *canzone* through its constitutive elements in *De vulgari eloquentia* (II, IX, 2–3), he opposes *cantio* as unit of sense (*sententia*) to *stantiae* as purely metrical units:

> And here you must know that this word [*stanza*] was coined solely for the purpose of discussing poetic technique, so that the object in which the whole art of the *canzone* was enshrined should be called a stanza, that is, a capacious storehouse or receptacle for the art in its entirety. *For just as the* canzone *is the lap of its subject-matter, so the stanza enlaps its whole technique*, and the latter stanzas of the poem should never aspire to add some new technical device, but should only dress themselves in the same garb as the first. (emphasis mine)

> (Et circa hoc sciendum est quod vocabulum [stantia] per solius artis respectum inventum est, videlicet ut in qua tota cantionis ars esset contenta, illud diceretur stantia, hoc est mansio capax sive receptaculum totois artis. Nam quemadmodum cantio est gremium totius sententiae, sic stantia totam artem ingremiat; nec licet aliquid artis sequentibus adrogare, sed solam artem antecedentis induere.)

Dante thus conceives of the structure of the *canzone* as founded on the relation between an essentially semantic, global unit ("the lap of the whole meaning") and essentially metrical, partial units ("enlaps the whole technique").

One of the first consequences of this position of the poem in an essential disjunction between sound and sense (marked by the possibility of enjambment) is the decisive importance of the end of the poem. The verse's syllables and accents can be counted; its synaloephae and caesuras can be noted; its anomalies and regularities can be catalogued. But the verse is, in every case, a unit that finds its *principium individuationis* only at the end, that defines itself only at the point at which it ends. I have elsewhere suggested that the word *versure*, from the Latin term indicating the point at which the plow turns around at the end of the furrow, be given to this essential trait of the verse, which—perhaps on account of its obviousness—has remained nameless among the moderns. Medieval treatises, by contrast, constantly draw attention to it. The fourth book of *Laborintus* thus registers *finalis terminatio* among the verse's essential elements, alongside *membrorum distincto* and *sillabarum numeratio*. And the author of the Munich *Ars* does not confuse the end of the poem (which he calls *pausatio*) with rhyme, but rather defines it as its source or condition of possibility: "the end is the source of consonance" (*est autem pausatio fons consonantiae*).

Only from this perspective is it possible to understand the singular prestige, in Provençal and Stilnovist poetry, of that very special poetic institution, the unrelated rhyme, called *rim'estrampa* by *Las leys d'amors* and *clavis* by Dante. If rhyme marked an antagonism between sound and sense by virtue of the noncorrespondence between homophony and meaning, here rhyme, absent from the point at which it was expected, momentarily allows the two series to interfere with each other in the semblance of a coincidence. I say "semblance," for if it is true that the lap of the whole technique here seems to break its metrical closure in marking the lap of sense, the unrelated rhyme nevertheless refers to a rhyme-fellow in the successive strophe and, therefore, does nothing more than bring metrical structure to the metastrophic level. This is why in Arnaut's hands it evolves almost naturally into word-rhyme, making possible the stupendous mechanism of the sestina. For word-rhyme is above all a point of undecidability between an essentially asemantic element (homophony) and an essentially semantic element (the word). The sestina is the poetic form that elevates the unrelated rhyme to the status of supreme compositional canon and seeks, so to speak, to incorporate the element of sound into the very lap of sense.

But it is time to confront the subject I announced and define the practice that modern works of poetics and meter have not considered: the end of the poem insofar as it is the ultimate formal structure perceptible in a poetic text. There have been inquiries into the *incipit* of poetry (even if they remain insufficient). But studies of the end of the poem, by contrast, are almost entirely lacking.

We have seen how the poem tenaciously lingers and sustains itself in the tension and difference between sound and sense, between the metrical series and the syntactical series. But what happens at the point at which the poem ends? Clearly, here there can be no opposition between a metrical limit and a semantic limit. This much follows simply from the trivial fact that there can be no enjambment in the final verse of a poem. This fact is certainly trivial; yet it implies consequences that are as perplexing as they are necessary. For if poetry is defined precisely by the possibility of enjambment, it follows that the last verse of a poem is not a verse.

Does this mean that the last verse trespasses into prose? For now let us leave this question unanswered. I would like, however, at least to call attention to the absolutely novel significance that Raimbaut d'Aurenga's "No sai que s'es" acquires from this perspective. Here the end of every strophe, and especially the end of the entire unclassifiable poem, is distinguished by the unexpected irruption of prose—an irruption that, *in extremis,* marks the epiphany of a necessary undecidability between prose and poetry.

Suddenly it is possible to see the inner necessity of those poetic institutions, like the *tornada* or the envoi, that seem solely destined to announce and almost declare the end of the poem, as if the end needed these institutions, as if for poetry the end implied a catastrophe and loss of identity so irreparable as to demand the deployment of very special metrical and semantic means.

This is not the place to give an inventory of these means or to conduct a phenomenology of the end of the poem (I am thinking, for example, of the particular intention with which Dante marks the end of each of the three books of the *Divine Comedy* with the word *stelle*, or of the rhymes in dissolved verses of Leopardi's poetry that intervene to stress the end of the strophe or the poem). What is essential is that the poets seem conscious of the fact that here there lies something like a decisive crisis for the poem, a genuine *crise de vers* in which the poem's very identity is at stake.

Hence the often cheap and even abject quality of the end of the poem. Proust once observed, with reference to the last poems of *Les fleurs du mal*, that the poem seems to be suddenly ruined and to lose its breath ("it stops short," he writes, "almost falls flat . . . despite everything, it seems that something has been shortened, is out of breath"). Think of "Le cygne," such a tight and heroic composition, which ends with the verse "Aux captifs, aux vaincues ... à bien d'autres encore!" (Of those who are captive or defeated ... and of many more others!) Concerning a different poem of Baudelaire's, Walter Benjamin noted that it "suddenly interrupts itself, giving one the impression—doubly surprising in a sonnet—of something fragmentary." The disorder of the last verse is an index of the structural relevance to the economy of the poem of the event I have called "the end of the poem." As if the poem as a formal structure would not and could not end, as if the possibility of the end were radically withdrawn from it, since the end would imply a poetic impossibility: the exact coincidence of sound and sense. At the point in which sound is about to be ruined in the abyss of sense, the poem looks for shelter in suspending its own end in a declaration, so to speak, of the state of poetic emergency.

In light of these reflections I would like to examine a passage in *De vulgari eloquentia* in which Dante seems, at least implicitly, to pose the problem of the end of poetry. The passage is to be found in Book II, where the poet treats the organization of rhymes in the *canzone* (XIII, 7–8). After defining the unrelated rhyme (which someone suggests should be called *clavis*), the text states: "The endings of the last verses are most beautiful if they fall into silence together with the rhymes" (*Pulcherrime tamen se habent ultimorum carminum desinentiae, si cum rithmo in silentium cadunt*). What is this falling into silence of the poem? What is beauty that falls? And what is left of the poem after its ruin?

If poetry lives in the unsatisfied tension between the semiotic and the semantic series alone, what happens at the moment of the end, when the opposition of the two series is no longer possible? Is there here, finally, a point of coincidence in which the poem, as "lap of the entire meaning," joins itself to its metrical element to pass definitively into prose? The mystical marriage of sound and sense could, then, take place.

Or, on the contrary, are sound and sense now forever separated without any possible contact, each eternally on its own side, like the two sexes in Vigny's poem? In this case, the poem would leave behind it only an empty space in which, according to Mallarmé's phrase, truly *rien n'aura lieu que le lieu*.

Everything is complicated by the fact that in the poem there are not, strictly speaking, two series or lines in parallel flight. Rather, there is but one line that is simultaneously traversed by the semantic current and the semiotic current. And between the flowing of these two currents lies the sharp interval obstinately maintained by poetic *mechanē*. (Sound and sense are not two substances but two intensities, two *tonoi* of the same linguistic substance.) And the poem is like the *katechon* in Paul's Second Epistle to the Thessalonians (2:7–8): something that slows and delays the advent of the Messiah, that is, of him who, fulfilling the time of poetry and uniting its two eons, would destroy the poetic machine by hurling it into silence. But what could be the aim of this theological conspiracy about language? Why so much ostentation to maintain, at any cost, a difference that succeeds in guaranteeing the space of the poem only on condition of depriving it of the possibility of a lasting accord between sound and sense?

Let us now reread what Dante says about the most beautiful way to end a poem, the place in which the last verses fall, rhymed, in silence. We know that for him it is a matter of a rule. Think, for instance, of the envoi of "Così nel mio parlar voglio esser aspro." Here the first verse ends with an absolutely unrelated rhyme, which coincides (and certainly not by chance) with the word that names the supreme poetic intention: *donna*, "lady." This unrelated rhyme, which seems to anticipate a point of coincidence between sound and sense, is followed by four verses, linked in couplets according to the rhyme that Italian metrical tradition calls *baciata* ("kissed"):

> Canzon, vattene dritto a quella donna
> che m'ha ferito il core e che m'invola
> quello ond'io ho più gola,
> e dàlle per lo cor d'una saetta;
> ché bell'onor s'acquista in far vendetta.

> (Poem, go straight to that woman who
> has wounded my heart and stolen from
> me what I most hunger for, and strike
> her heart with an arrow, for one gains
> great honor in taking revenge.)

It is as if the verse at the end of the poem, which was now to be irreparably ruined in sense, linked itself closely to its rhyme-fellow and, laced in this way, chose to dwell with it in silence.

This would mean that the poem falls by once again marking the opposition between the semiotic and the semantic, just as sound seems forever consigned to sense and sense returned forever to sound. The double intensity animating language does not die away in a final comprehension; instead it collapses into silence, so to speak, in an endless falling. The poem thus reveals the goal of its proud strategy: to let language finally communicate itself, without remaining unsaid in what is said.

(Wittgenstein once wrote that "philosophy should really only be poeticized" [*Philosophie dürfte man eigentlich nur dichten*]. Insofar as it acts as if sound and sense coincided in its discourse, philosophical prose may risk falling into banality; it may risk, in other words, lacking thought. As for poetry, one could say, on the contrary, that it is threatened by an excess of tension and thought. Or, rather, paraphrasing Wittgenstein, that poetry should really only be philosophized.)

Appendix

An Enigma Concerning
the Basque Woman

In the preface (or, rather, the extremely long *razo*) added to the
second edition of *Il ricordo della Basca* in 1963, Antonio Delfini defines his story as "a pastiche that no one understood." He then
warns his readers against the temptation of asking, "Why a Basque
woman? Who is she? What does she mean?"

The darkest point in the story is certainly the poem in a foreign
language that, like a final seal, closes the *trobar clus* of the story's final pages:

> Ene izar maitea
> ene charmagarria
> ichilik zure ikhustera
> yten nitzaitu leihora;
> koblatzen dudalarik,
> zande lokharturik:
> gabazko ametsa bezala
> ene kantua zaïtzula.

That these incomprehensible verses might somehow help to answer
the bothersome reader's questions is suggested by their strategic position at the end of the work. It is also implied by the fact that
when the author (consciously alluding to the passage in the *Vita
nuova* in which Dante refers to the epiphany of Beatrice) tells the
story, in his *razo*, of his first encounter with the fifteen-year-old girl

"I came to call the Basque woman," he characterizes her precisely through a reference to her language: she spoke with her brother "in a language of such touching delicacy that when I heard it, my heart seemed to want to put an end to its own beating, leaving things suspended forever in that moment" (p. 92). (A little later, the author seeks to understand the words of the two youths, and he then comes so close to them that he can "almost touch them" [p. 94]. But he can gather only the word "entonces," Castillian for "at that time," which is the very *in illo tempore* of myth.) The Basque woman appears through the sweetness of an unknown language, and she disappears in the ungraspable murmur of words in a foreign language. Who is the Basque woman? And why is she obstinately characterized by an impenetrable "speaking in tongues"?

A first answer is implicit precisely in the incomprehensible nature of the verses at issue. The story suggests several times that the Basque woman is that which is so inner and present that it can never be remembered ("I would like her to be so close to me that a forced memory would not give me even her image" [p. 202]). What, then, is more inner and immemorable than a speaking in tongues, that is, a language in which the spirit is joined with the voice without the mediation of meaning (cf. 1 Corinthians 14:2, "He that speaketh in an unknown tongue speaketh not unto men, but unto God: for no man understandeth him; howbeit in the spirit he speaketh mysteries")?

Following a tenacious troubadour and Stilnovist intention that makes of a female *senhal* the symbol of the language of poetry, the Basque woman would therefore be the cipher of this originary and immediate status of language, in which language is, as in Dante's "maternal speech" (*parlar materno*), what is "unique and first in the mind" and with respect to which no knowledge and grammar are possible. Insofar as he experiences this immediate dwelling of the word in the beginning, the poet cannot "say anything that has something to say" (p. 211); he is absolutely without words before language.

If the Basque is the figure of this immediate event of language, why then is the story called "Remembrance of the Basque Woman"?

And why is the Basque woman not merely lost but, rather, "a woman eternally vanished" (p. 206)?

Contradicting himself in this way, Delfini discreetly gestures toward the other Basque woman of twentieth-century Italian literature, who clearly constitutes the example here: Manuelita Etchegarray, the Creole woman of "Dualismo" in Dino Campana's *Canti orfici*, whose name is clearly of Basque origin. Against the naive faith in poetic immediacy, Campana (who formulates his poetics here, as Gianfranco Contini has observed) asserts the dualism and bilingualism that, for him, constitute the experience of poetry: memory and immediacy, the letter and the spirit, thought and presence. Poetry is always divided between an impossibility of thinking ("I did not think, I did not think of you: I have never thought of you") and the compulsion to think ("I lost you then, Manuelita . . . I remember, I went into the library"), between an incapacity to remember in the perfect, amorous adhesion to the present and the memory that wells up precisely in the impossibility of this love. This inner divergence is the dictation of poetry. As in the song by the troubadour Folquet de Marselha, the poet cannot help remembering in his song the very thing that he would like only to forget there ("In singing I recall what I am trying, in singing, to forget").

Hence what Delfini calls "the irremediable tragedy of this memory" (p. 211). The experience of poetic language (that is, of love) is wholly contained in the fracture between an immemorable presence and the necessity of remembering. The language of poetry is not, therefore, a perfect speaking in tongues in which this fracture is healed, just as, despite its tension toward the absolute, human language cannot leap over mediation of meaning and resolve itself without residue in a "speaking in tongues." The disappearance of the Basque woman is eternal, since she is eternally missing in the languages of men, which bear witness to her in the Babelic discord of their many idioms alone.

If this is true, then the poem with which the story ends cannot simply be a speaking in tongues, a *glossolalia*. Rather, it must in some way bear witness to the radical *diglossia* of the poetic experience. The work of a friend of mine, who is a Basque specialist, con-

firms this hypothesis. It has shown beyond the shadow of a doubt
that, far from constituting a glossolalic invention (as in certain stories by Tommaso Landolfi), the poem is in fact a *cobla* in pure
Basque. "The poem," my friend informs us,

> is written in a perfectly comprehensible northern Basque. Naturally it
> is not a Basque that respects the rules established by the present *Real
> Academia vasca*; it employs the subjunctive and other grammatical
> forms that are no longer in use. The only trait that can be defined as
> incorrect is the spelling *ichilik* in v. 3, which should be emended to *ix-
> ilik*; moreover, the term *koblatzen* (v. 5), from "copla," no longer means
> "to find," that is, "to compose poetry." On the basis of these charac-
> teristics it is possible to date the poem between the seventeenth and
> the eighteenth centuries.

And here is the translation done by my friend, which I translate
from Spanish:

> My beloved star,
> my enchantress,
> I come, mute, to look at you;
> for me you leave by the window.
> When I find a poem,
> you are falling asleep—
> may my song be for you
> like the dream of the night.

At this point, it is obvious that the lines that immediately precede
the poem in Delfini's story can be said to paraphrase it; and it is
therefore clear that Delfini must have known the poem's meaning,
although it is unlikely he was its author. How he procured the text
and the linguistic competence to understand the poem is a problem we leave to future biographers. For now it suffices to have been
able to contribute in some way to the understanding of an enigma
(or, rather, a "pastiche") that still remains to be fully solved.

∿

In March 1993, after this article had been published in the issue
of the journal *Marka* that is devoted to Delfini, I received a letter

from Bernard Simeone, a French professor of Italian literature, in which he wrote:

> I had occasion to read your text, "An Enigma Concerning the Basque Woman," in the company of a Basque friend from Ustarritz, who immediately recognized the poem cited by Delfini. It is a text from the "Vicomte de Belzunce," written at the end of the sixteenth or the beginning of the seventeenth century. His translation is slightly different from that suggested by your friend, the Basque specialist. It reads:
>
> > My beloved star,
> > my charming one,
> > in silence to contemplate you
> > do I approach the window.
> > When the poem is born on my lips,
> > stay sleeping:
> > let my song be to you
> > like a dream in the night.
>
> Verses 4 and 6 assume a different and more coherent meaning in this possible version: it is the poet who approaches the window, and the sixth verse is an exhortation (an imperative). This poem, which is by now almost a popular song, can be found in various Basque anthologies that I could direct you to, if it interests you.

It is still the case that the poem is an important piece in the puzzle of Delfini's poetics, not only because of its poetry/dream equation, but also and above all because of the play it suggests between real language and imaginary language. But the poem may also cast new light on some of Landolfi's inventions (like the unintelligible composition at the center of *Dialogo dei massimi sistemi*, whose real character will now have to be verified; Delfini and Landolfi both frequented Florentine cafés, and the young Landolfi's passion for exotic languages is well known). It may, moreover, begin a new historiographical chapter in the history of twentieth-century Italian poetics. In particular, the claims put forward by the character "Y" would, from this perspective, assume an unmistakably Delfinian quality (without infringing on the question of priority: Landolfi's *Dialogo* is from 1935).

B   The Hunt for Language

In the Bible, the exemplary hunter is the giant Nemrod, the same one to whom tradition attributes the project of the tower of Babel, whose summit was to touch the sky. The author of Genesis defines him as "a mighty hunter before the Lord" (10:9) (or rather "against the Lord," as we read in the older Latin, "Itala" version), and this quality was so essential that it became a proverb ("wherefore it is said, Even as Nemrod the mighty hunter before the Lord").

In *Inferno*, XXXI, Dante punishes Nemrod for his "ill thought" (*mal coto*) with the loss of meaningful language ("for every language is to him as his is to others, which is known to none" [*ché cosè a lui ciascun linguaggio / come'l suo ad altrui, ch'a nullo è noto*]): he can only utter senseless sounds (*Raphél may améch zabì almi*) or, as a hunter, sound his horn ("Stupid soul, keep to your horn and with that vent yourself" [*Anima sciocca / tienti col corno, e con quel ti disfoga*]).[1]

What did Nemrod hunt? And why is his hunt "against God"? If the punishment of Babel was the confusion of languages, it is likely that Nemrod's hunt had to do with an artificial improvement of the one human language that was to grant reason unlimited power. Dante at least suggests this much when, in characterizing the perfidy of the giants, he speaks of an "instrument of the mind" (*argomento della mente*) (*Inferno*, XXXI, 55).

Is it mere chance that in *De vulgari eloquentia* Dante also constantly presents his own search for the "illustrious vernacular" in terms of a hunt ("we are hunting down language" [I, XI, 1]; "what we are hunting for" [I, XV, 8]; "our hunting arms" [I, XVI, 2]) and that language is thus assimilated to a ferocious beast, a panther?

At the origins of the Italian literary tradition, the search for an illustrious poetic language is placed under the disturbing sign of Nemrod and his titanic hunt, almost as if to signify the mortal risk implicit in every search for language that seeks in some way to restore its originary splendor.

The "hunt for language" is both an antidivine arrogance that exalts the calculating power of the word and an amorous search that wants to remedy Babelic presumption. Every serious human effort in language must always confront this risk.

~

In Caproni's late poetry, these two themes are brought so close that they coincide in the idea of an obsessive and ferocious hunt whose object is language itself, a hunt that unites the biblical giant's challenge to the limits of language with Dante's pious veneration. The two aspects of human language (Nemrod's naming and the poet's amorous search) have now become indistinguishable. And the hunt is truly a mortal experience whose prey—speech—is a beast that, as Caproni says, "animates and kills" and that, "tame and atrocious," once again—for what is perhaps the last time—wears the speckled coat of Dante's panther (but a "nebulous panther," a "suicidal" panther).

Speech now turns to its own logical power; it says *itself* and, in this extreme poetic gesture, grasps only its own foolishness and appears only in its own dispersion. The "trumpet" that can be heard to "echo" in the interrupted music of the late Caproni is the last, muffled resonance of Nemrod's raving "high horn," of the "mighty hunter before the Lord."

C The Just Do Not Feed on Light

In May 1960, Paul Celan met Nelly Sachs for the first time. It was the Feast of the Ascension, and while the two poets were speaking in front of the cathedral ("we spoke of your God," Celan writes, "and I spoke against him") it seemed to them that a golden light shone from the water in which the façade was reflected. A few months later, the two friends met again in Paris, in Celan's home. "While we were speaking at our home for the second time about God, about your God, the one that is waiting for you, the golden light shone on the wall."

Years later, announcing to his friend the imminent publication of *Fadensonnen* (1968), Celan wrote: "Thank you for your lines, for the remembrance of that light. Yes, that light. You will find it named in my next collection, which is coming out in April, named—called by a Hebrew name." The poem at issue is the one that begins "Nah, im Aortenbogen":

> Nah, im Aortenbogen,
> Im Hellblut:
> das Hellwort.
>
> Mutter Rahel
> weint nicht mehr.
> Rübergetragen
> alles Geweinte.

Still, in den Kranzarterien,
unumschnürt:
Ziw, jenes Licht.[1]

(Near, in the aorta-arch,
in the bright blood: the
bright word. Mother Rahel
no longer cries. Everything
cried—carried over. Quiet,
in the coronary arteries,
untied: Ziw, that light.)

Ziw is the term with which the Kabbalists name the splendor of
the *Shekhina*, that is, the divine manifestation. And in the world
to come, the just feed on this light.

Two years later, the image of light returned as a keyword in the
next collection, *Lichtzwang*. But this time it was a matter of a "light
compulsion" that keeps human creatures, who are lost and hud-
dled as if in a wood, from touching themselves:

Wir lagen
schon tief in der Macchia, als du
endlich herankrochst.
Doch konnten wir nicht
hinüberdunkeln zu dir:
es herrschte
Lichtzwang.

(We were lying
deep in the macchia, by the time
you crept up at last.
But we could not
darken over to you:
light compulsion
reigned.)[2]

In January 1991, when Eugenio De Signoribus composed his
Belliche series, he, too, invoked something like a glimmer, a light.
According to a tradition still alive in Dante, "the form of light" is
identical to the divine substance and is the cipher of the perfect

transparency of a thinking that, in thinking itself, thinks all things. This light is now (since when?) fractured into a "hypocritical beacon" that lights up the night and in whose service there are "tinsel-wearers" and "prayer-predators" whose language balks at "following the course / of the common good," and a "defenseless, unredeemed light" that searches gropingly for its brothers in an inhospitable world:

> Luce inerme, irredenta luce
> che bruci nel mondo inospitale
>
> tra i solchi scellerati e i cancelli
> fissati dalla mente criminale . . .
>
> nell'angolo cieco o nel vuoto delle stanze
> tu sei, o nel pianto del luminìo campale . . .
>
> il faro ipocrita illumina le bande
> ma tu esisti, e cerchi i tuoi fratelli.
>
> (Defenseless, unredeemed light, you who
> burn in the inhospitable world, between the
> wicked furrows and gates fixed in the crim-
> inal mind . . . you are in the blind corner or
> the emptiness of rooms, or in the lament of
> the battle-field glare . . . the hypocritical
> beacon lights up the troops, but you exist
> and search for your brothers.)

The off-screen voice that speaks this completely profane light seems to come from nowhere—or from a television that someone has forgotten to turn off, a television that shows houses leveled to the ground, Iraq in flames, the "electrocuted stare" of children. Lost, sub- or para-human, like that of a just human being who has learned to fast on *Ziw*, this voice has realized the prophetic omen of *Assassinii*:

> Sopra la loro testa divisa
> possano uccelli e vermi parlare.
>
> (Above their divided head birds
> and worms can speak.)

The poet who, "in the evening of the century," speaks with this voice—a voice so lowly that it cannot be recognized, and so strong that it can barely be heard—knew how to name the "crooked face of the world." He is perhaps the greatest engaged poet of his generation, and the Italian poetry that is to come—the poetry that will, of course, have to fast on light—will be incessantly forced to confront him.

D Taking Leave of Tragedy

My friendship with Elsa Morante began twenty-two years ago, on the small train that travels through the Roman countryside from Piazzale Flaminio to Viterbo. Elsa was going to see her mother, who was recovering in a nursing home in Viterbo. Wilcock, whom I had met a few months before, had chosen that very day to introduce us. Elsa left us at the Viterbo train station, and we met up again an hour later. It was not easy for Elsa to see the ailing patient. Elsa's mother suffered from partial dementia following a serious form of arteriosclerosis, and she did not recognize her daughter. But in looking at her mother, Elsa had the impression of seeing herself in that face framed by tufts of white hair. She went away frightened. She told me years later that this was why she preferred to dye her prematurely graying hair. (In the Roman clinic where Elsa spent the last three years of her life, when she had not been dyeing her hair for some time and she sometimes momentarily seemed not to recognize me, I was reminded of our first meeting.)

From that day on, our intense, almost feverish friendship began. We saw each other every day, sometimes from morning till evening. Elsa was very free when she was not writing. In the morning we would have breakfast outside Rome, or on the old Via Attica, at the "I trenini" bistro; in the evening we would go to some restaurant in the center. In addition to younger friends, Pier Paolo

Pasolini, Sandro Penna, Natalia and Gabriele Baldini, and Cesare Garboli were also often present.

I was twenty-one years old then, and I will never forget the support—capricious but incomparable—that Elsa's friendship gave me. But if I ask myself now what it was that so struck me from the very first meeting, what it was that I always found in Elsa, I can only say: she was serious, wildly serious. I do not mean "serious" in the sense of someone who takes everything as true and with gravity. Even without taking account of her readings of the Indian classics, Elsa was very aware that the world is only appearance (remember the "subversive refrain" from *Il mondo salvato dai ragazzini?*). Her seriousness was instead that of someone who completely and unreservedly believes in Fiction and, therefore, means to say everything that it says. In *Alibi*, that extraordinary collection of poems that went almost unnoticed at the time of its publication in 1958 and that is in fact one of the great books of Italian postwar poetry, there is a poem that contains a precious key to Elsa's fantastic world. It is the one called "Alla favola" and begins, "I cover myself with you, Fiction / foolish garment" (*Di te, Finzione / mi cingo, / fatua veste*). This is why, given the two possible relationships to language—tragedy and comedy—Elsa instinctively adhered to the tragic one.

Ingeborg Bachmann (whom Elsa and I met and saw frequently a few years later and who truly resembled Elsa very much) once made this terrible confession: "Language is punishment. All things must enter into language and remain there according to the degree of their guilt." In this sense, the serious word is the one that never forgets that language is punishment and that we are all, in speaking or writing, suffering a punishment.

Is there redemption from this punishment? In a poem, Ingeborg turns to speech, to punishment itself, to ask for salvation: "Oh my speech, save me!" But for Elsa, there seems to be neither escape nor redemption from the punishment of language. When I told her, many years later, that I was writing a book called *Language and Death*, she commented: "Language and death? Language *is* death!" (*Il linguaggio e la morte? Il linguaggio è la morte!*)

This is why Elsa's work appears as one of the few truly tragic works in a literary tradition—the Italian tradition—that has remained so obstinately faithful to the antitragic intention of the *Divine Comedy*. But in Elsa (and this was perhaps her Christian inheritance), it is as if inside tragedy there were another tragedy that resisted it, such that the tragic conflict explodes, not between guilt and innocence but between two incommensurable punishments. Another poem from *Alibi* formulates the law that broke her heart in this way: "There is no Elysium outside limbo." As is well known, limbo is the place not of innocents but rather of those who have no other guilt than natural guilt, of those infants who could not have been submitted to the punishment of language and to whom Elsa looked lovingly for her whole life. The baptism of the Verb cancels this natural guilt, but it cancels it only through another, more atrocious punishment. But in Elsa it is as if, at a certain point, the creature from limbo lifted its fragile arm against the historical tragedy of a language in a hopeless gesture, in a silent confrontation whose outcome cannot easily be understood.

I often asked myself in the last months, when the tragic part of Elsa's life had grown beyond every measure, whether there was not an antitragic gleam in her, whether her tragedy was not, in some way, an *antitragic tragedy*. Every tragedy certainly projects a comic shadow, and whoever knew Elsa remembers the incredible little songs that only she knew and with which she could make her friends laugh if she wanted (there is a trace of them in the distracted refrains with which she liked to fill up her novels). But this is not what I mean. Rather, it is sometimes as if Elsa adhered so tenaciously to tragic fiction that it opened up a path beyond itself, toward something that is no longer tragic (even if it also cannot be called comic). In this path, without punishment or redemption, we momentarily gaze upon pure Fiction before demons bring it to Hell or angels carry it away to the sky. And this moment—in which fiction is seen and speech expiated—is a departure from tragedy. Only at this point does Elsa's poetry show its shining phoenix, its eternal ash.

Reference Matter

Notes

1. Comedy

1. The inability to give even a coherent explanation of the poem's title is common to almost all the medieval commentators, from Pietro Alighieri to Jacopo della Lana and the Anonymous of Florence. As Erich Auerbach has noted, however, Benvenuto da Imola stands out among all others for having first formulated the argument—so often repeated by modern critics—that Dante's poem is, as to its material, at once tragedy, satire, and comedy ("hic est tragoedia, satyra et comoedia"), yet owes its title to stylistic considerations ("dico quod auctor voluit vocare librum Comoedia a stylo infimo et vulgari"). See *Benvenuti de Rambaldis de Imola Comentum super Dantis Aligherij nunc primum integre in lucem editum* (Florence: G. Barbera, 1887), 1: 18–19.

2. "I do not know how to explain the facts except by supposing that Dante must have made the choice of the title fairly early on. A poetic narration in the high style was at that point and always continued to be for him tragedy; and, therefore, no work deserved that designation more than Virgil's poem. But when confronted with Virgil, Dante is overcome with feelings of reverence and admiration, feelings he attributes to Sordello and Statius in the *Purgatorio*. If Virgil's work was therefore a tragedy, Dante's own could only be a comedy. He was, moreover, determined to write in the vernacular; and I thus conclude that he did not yet have as high an opinion of the vernacular as he was to have in the *Convivio*, even if he had already rejected the strict notions of the *Vita nova*" (Pio Rajna, "Il titolo del poema dantesco," *Studi danteschi* 4 [1921]: 35). It is unfor-

tunate to see such an unsatisfying explanation in the recent *Enciclopedia dantesca* (see "Commedia"). On the problem of *Commedia*'s title, see also M. Porena, "Il titolo della Commedia," Rend. Acc. Lincei, 6-IX-1933; F. Mazzoni, "L'epistola a Cangrande," *Studi Monteverdi* (Modena), 1959 (now in *Contributi di filologia dantesca* [Florence: Sansoni, 1966]); and Manlio Pastore-Stocchi, "Mussato e la tragedia," in *Dante e la cultura veneta* (Firenze: L. S. Olschki, 1966). On Dante's "comic style," see Alfredo Schiaffini, "A proposito dello stile comico di Dante," in *Momenti di storia della lingua italiana* (Rome: Studium, 1953); and, above all, the observations in Gianfranco Contini, "Un'interpretazione di Dante" and "Filologia e esegesi dantesca," now both collected in *Un'idea di Dante* (Turin: Einaudi, 1976).

3. Erich Auerbach, *Mimesis: The Representation of Reality in the Western World*, trans. Willard R. Trask (Princeton, N.J.: Princeton University Press, 1953), p. 186.

4. Ibid., p. 187.

5. Giovanni Boccaccio, *Il commento alla Divina Commedia e gli altri scritti intorno a Dante*, ed. D. Guerri (Bari: Laterza, 1918), I: 115. The Italian text reads as follows: "Che adunque diremo delle obiezioni fatte? Credo, conciosiacosaché oculatissimo uomo, lui non avere avuto riguardo alle parti che nella commedia si contengono, ma al tutto, e da quello avere il suo libro dinominato, figurativamente parlando. Il tutto della commedia è (per quello che per Plauto e per Terenzio, che furono poeti comici, si può comprehendere): che la commedia abbia turbolento principio e pieno di romori e di discordie, e poi l'ultima parte di quella finisca in pace e in tranquillità. Al qual tutto è ottimamente conforme il libro presente: percioché egli incomincia da' dolori e dalle turbazioni infernali e finisce nel riposo e nella pace e nella gloria, la quale hanno i beati in vita eterna. E questo dee poter bastare a fare che così fatto nome si possa di ragione convenire a questo libro."

6. *De vulgari eloquentia*, ed. and trans. Stephen Botterill (Cambridge, Eng.: Cambridge University Press, 1996), II, IV, 8, pp. 58–59.

7. Ibid., II, VIII, 8, pp. 71–73.

8. Dante's lexicographic sources have been indicated by Paget Toynbee, *Dante Studies and Researches* (London: Methuen, 1972) and Rajna, "Il titolo del poema dantesco." That Dante scholarship has searched for the poet's sources in only lexicographic and grammatical treatises is, however, to our eyes one of the reasons why it has been unable to develop a more profound understanding of the problem of the poem's comic title.

9. *Dantis Alaghierii Epistolae; The Letters of Dante*, ed. and trans. Paget Toynbee (Oxford: Oxford University Press, 1966), Letter X, §10, p. 175; trans. p. 200.

10. Dante Alighieri, *The Divine Comedy, Inferno*, trans. Charles Singleton (Princeton, N.J.: Princeton University Press, 1970), XX, 113, pp. 210–11. All subsequent references to the Comedy are to the Singleton bilingual edition and translation: *Purgatorio* (Princeton, N.J.: Princeton University Press, 1973); *Paradiso* (Princeton, N.J.: Princeton University Press, 1975).

11. Diomedes, in Heinrich Keil, *Grammatici latini ex recensione Henrici Keilii* (Leipzig: B. G. Teubner, 1855), 1: 482. The distinction between *genus activum* (that is, *sine poetae interlocutione*), *genus enarrativum* (in which only the poet speaks), and *genus commune* can be found in Isidore (*Etymologiae*, VIII, 7, 11: "Apud poetas autem tres characteres esse dicendi: unum, in quo tantum poeta loquitur, ut est in libris Vergilii Gerorgicorum; alium dramaticum, in quo nusquam poeta loquitur, ut est in comediis et tragediis; tertium mixtum, ut est in Aeneide. Nam poeta illic et introductae personae loquuntur"). On this classification see Ernst Robert Curtius's observations in "Excursus V" (dedicated to late ancient literary studies), in *European Literature and the Latin Middle Ages*, trans. Willard R. Trask (Princeton, N.J.: Princeton University Press, 1953), pp. 436–45.

12. *Rhetorica ad Herennium*, IV, 8: "Sunt . . . tria genera, quae genera nos figuras appellamus, in quibus omnis ratio non vitiosa consumitur: unam gravem, alteram mediocrem, tertiam extenuata vocamus. Gravis est, quae constat ex verborum gravium magna et ornata constructione; mediocris est, quae constat ex humiliore, neque tamen ex infima et pervulgatissima verborum dignitate; attenuata est, quae demissa est usque ad usitatissimam puri sermonis consuetudinem." For the medieval development of these ideas (of which an example can be found in Isidore's theory of the three *modi dicendi*, in *Etymologiae*, II, 17) and for their relation to the distinction between tragedy and comedy, see Wilhelm Cloetta, *Beiträge zur Literaturgeschichte des Mittelalters und der Renaissance* (Halle: Niemeyer, 1890), 1: 24–25; and Edmond Faral, *Les arts poétiques du XII et XIII siècle* (Paris: Champion, 1962), pp. 86ff.

13. In *De vulgari eloquentia* (II, IV, 5), Dante still holds to the prevalent tripartition and also lists the elegy alongside tragedy and comedy. In Matthew of Vendôme's *Ars versificatoria*, comedy appears as the third style, after tragedy and satire, and before the elegy: "Tertia surrepit co-

moedia, cotidiano habitu, humilito capite, nullius festivitatis pratendens delicias" (Faral, *Les arts poétiques,* p. 153). Dante's oldest commentators also know four poetic styles. In this context, the letter to Cangrande marks a passage from a tripartition (or quadropartition) to a juxtaposition, a passage for which precedents cannot easily be found.

14. "And there are other kinds of poetical narration, such as the pastoral poem, the elegy, the satire, and the votive song, as may be gathered from Horace in *The Art of Poetry*; but of these we need say nothing at present" (*Sunt et alia genera narrationum poëticarum, scilicet carmen bucolicum, elegia, satira, et sententia votiva, ut etiam per Oratium patere potest in sua poetria; sed de istis ad praesens nihil dicendum est*) (*Dantis Alaghierii Epistolae,* §10, p. 177; trans. p. 201). It should be noted that in the treatment of comedy and tragedy contained in Aristotle's *Poetics,* the two genres are not explicitly opposed to each other. The only passage in which Aristotle explicitly opposes tragedy and comedy is *De generatione et corruptione* (315b), in which we read the comment, made in passing, that "with the same letters it is possible to write both tragedies and comedies." In his commentary on this passage, St. Thomas writes as follows: "Et ponit exemplum in sermonibus quorum prima principia indivisibilia sunt litterae: ex eisdem autem litteris, transmutatis secundum ordinem aut positionem, fiunt diversi sermones, puta comoedia, quae est sermo de rebus urbanis, et tragoedia, qua est sermo de rebus bellicis." *Sancti Thomae Aquinatis, doctoris angelica: Opera omnia* (Rome: Ex Typographica Polyglotta S. C. de Propaganda Fide, 1886), 3: 275.

15. "Comica nonne vides ipsum reprehendere verba." Dante Alighieri, *Ecl.,* I, 52.

16. See Auerbach's observations, which show that the expression "locutio vulgaris, in qua et muliercule communicant," which Dante uses in the letter to Cangrande, cannot refer to the use of the Italian language: "It is difficult to attribute such an idea to Dante, who defended the noble dignity of the vernacular in his *De vulgari eloquentia,* who was himself the founder of the elevated style in the vernacular through his *canzoni,* and who had finished the Comedy at the time when he wrote his letter to Cangrande." Auerbach, *Mimesis,* p. 186.

17. Giovanni's expression is: "Praetera nullus, quos inter es agmine sextus / nec quem consequeris coleo, sermone forensi / descripsit." See *La corrispondenza poetica di Dante e Giovanni di Virgilio e l'ecloga di Giovanni al Mussatto,* ed. Giuseppe Albini (Florence: L. S. Olschki, 1963).

18. " . . . di questa commedia, id est istius operis, quod auctor vocavit

comoediam non tam ratione materiae, quam styli vulgaris humilis" (see Benvenuti Rambaldis de Imola, *Comentum*, p. 556). Contini, the author of magnificent remarks on Dante's "comic" style, implicitly admits the insufficiency of formal motivations, repeating Benvenuto's thesis of the "name with an infamous origin": "In this place in which all tradition is summed up, in this extraordinary institution of thematic and tonal mixtures . . . the stroke of intellectual genius is to have begun at the lowest level" (Contini, "Un'interpretazione di Dante," p. 104). On Dante's comic style, see also Schiaffini's study, "A proposito dello stile comico di Dante," which shows how, from the lexical point of view, idioms (such as *introcque*) and "humble" words (such as *mamma, gregge, femmina, corpo*) are, all things considered, of little importance.

19. *Dantis Alaghierii Epistolae*, §8, p. 124; trans. p. 200.

20. Herman the German attempted to translate the *Poetics* from the Arabic version before 1250; but in 1256 he declared that his attempt had failed on account of insurmountable difficulties and that he preferred to translate Averroes's Middle Commentary ("tantam inveni difficultatem proper disconvenenciam modi metrificandi in greco cum modo metrificandi in arabico et propter vocabulorum obscuritatem"; see E. Franceschini, "La poetica di Aristotele nel sec. XIII," *Atti dell'Ist. veneto di scienze, lettere e arti* [1934–35]). William of Moerbeke's Latin translation was completed in 1278 and is reproduced in vol. 33 of *Aristoteles Latinus*, ed. E. Franceschini and L. Minio-Paluello (Bruges-Paris: Brouwer, 1953).

21. "Komodia autem est, sicut diximus, mutatio peiorem quidem, non tamen secundum omnem malitiam, sed turpis est quod risile particula; nam risile est peccatum aliquod et turpitudo non dolorosa et non corruptiva." *Aristoteles Latinus*, 30: 8.

22. Ibid., p. 16. It is in this passage of Aristotle's *Poetics* (52b, 35) that one may presumably seek the remote origin of the medieval characterization of tragedy and comedy according to the happy beginning / unhappy ending opposition. It should be noted that Aristotle does not say that the misfortune / good fortune inversion is comical, but says only that it is antitragic (*atragodotaton*, which William translates as *intragodotatissimum*).

23. *Aristoteles stagiritae omnia quae extant opera cum Averrois cordubensis . . . commentaris* (Venice: n.p., 1552), 2: 91.

24. Ibid., pp. 91–92.

25. "Aliqui tamen introducunt in illis scenis tragicis imitationem vitiorum et scelerum simul cum rebus laudabilis, cum habeant quid

peripetiae. Verum vituperare vitia est potius comoediae proprium quam tragoedia." Ibid., p. 91.

26. *De vulgari eloquentia,* I, IV, 4–5, pp. 8–9.

27. Kurt von Fritz, *Antike und Moderne Tragödie* (Berlin: de Gruyter, 1962).

28. Dante, *Divine Comedy, Paradiso,* VII, 85, pp. 76–77.

29. On the distinction between natural justice and personal justice, see Charles S. Singleton's extremely acute observations in *Journey to Beatrice* (Baltimore: Johns Hopkins University Press, 1958), pp. 222–53. The distinction between natural guilt and personal guilt elaborated by the Church Fathers corresponds to Fritz's distinction between objective guilt and subjective guilt.

30. "Fuit enim peccatum Adae in homine, quod est in natura; et in illo qui vocatus est Adam, quod est in persona. Est tamen peccatum quod quisque . . . " St. Anselm, *De conceptu virg. et de orig. peccato,* in Migne, *Patrologia Latina,* 158: 433.

31. "Ergo in eis (sc. pueris) est aliquid peccatum. Sed non peccatum actuale, quia non habent puer usum liberi arbitir, sine quo nihil imputatur homini ad peccatum. . . . Necesse est igitur dicere quod in eis sit peccatum per originem traductum." Divi Thomae Aq., *Summa contra gentiles* (Rome, 1927), p. 639.

32. St. Augustine, *Concerning the City of God, Against the Pagans,* trans. Henry Bettenson (New York, 1972), p. 582.

33. St. Augustine, *De civitate Dei,* XIV, 20.

34. St. Augustine, *City of God,* p. 582.

35. "Si de illo peccato non fusset satisfactum per mortem Christi, adhuc essemus filii ire natura, natura scilicet depravata." Dante, *De monarchia,* 2, II, 2–3.

36. Divi Thomae, *Summa contra gentiles,* p. 657.

37. St. Thomas, *De malo,* 9. 4, a.6, ad 4. Heretical movements such as Adamism, which, starting in the thirteenth century, preached free love and the impeccability of the perfect Christian, are directed against this contradiction in Christian theology, which keeps alive *natural* guilt after redemption, if only in the form of a *poena.*

38. "Est autem paene totus in affectione, licet in fine pathos habeat, ubi abscessus Aeneae gignit dolorem. Sane totus in consiliis et subtilitatibus est: nam paene comicus stilus est: nec mirum, ubi de amore tractatur." Servius, regarding Book IV of the *Aeneid*; see *Servianorum in Verg. Carmina Com.* (Oxford: Oxford University Press, 1965), 2: 247.

39. On the essence of courtly love and Dante's relation to it, see Roger Dragonetti's extremely acute observations in "L'épisode de Francesca selon la convention courtoise," in *Aux frontières du langage poétique (Études sur Dante, Mallarmé, Valéry)*, vol. 10 (Gent: Romanica Gandensia, 1961).

40. Dante, *Divine Comedy, Purgatorio*, XVII, 94, pp. 184–85.

41. Ibid., XVIII, 34–69, pp. 190–93.

42. Ibid., XXX, 78, pp. 330–31.

43. Ibid., XXXI, 43–45, pp. 340–41.

44. Ibid., XXXI, 64, p. 342.

45. Ibid., XXXI, 68, pp. 342–43.

46. Dante Alighieri, *Opere minori*, ed. Cesare Vasoli and Domenico De Robertis (Milan: Ricciardi, 1995), vol. II, 2, *Convivio*, 4, XIX, 8–10, pp. 742–43; *Dante's "Il Convivio" (The Banquet)*, trans. Richard H. Lansing (New York: Garland, 1990), p. 205.

47. Dante, *Opere minori*, vol. II, 1, *Convivio*, 3, VIII, 10; *Dante's "Il Convivio" (The Banquet)*, p. III. Translation slightly modified.

48. On the conception and practice of penitential humiliation in the twelfth century and their influence on the juridical theory of crime as sin, see Mario Dal Pra's remarks in Peter Abelard, *Conosci te stesso, o Etica*, ed. Mario Dal Pra (Florence: La Nuova Italia, 1976), pp. 86–87.

49. Singleton, *Journey to Beatrice*, pp. 205–21. It is curious that Singleton, who identified Matelda as the natural justice enjoyed by man in Paradise, did not draw the consequences of this identification as far as the theory of love was concerned. If Matelda is natural justice, she does not simply signify the triple subjection of nature to reason; she is also necessarily the figure of Edenic love, that is, of the *voluntarius usus sine ardoris illecebroso stimulo*.

50. See Barnes, "Dante's Matelda," *Italian Studies* 28 (1973).

51. *Epict. Ench.*, XVII: "Remember that you are like an actor in the part that the playwright wanted to assign you: brief, if it is brief; long, if it is long. If he wants you to perform the part of the beggar, perform it well. Do the same for the party of a lame person, a magistrate, or an ordinary citizen. For your task is to perform well the character that has been assigned to you; to choose the character is that of another." *Epict. Diss.*, I, XXIX, 39: "Is it perhaps in your power to choose a subject? You have been assigned a certain body, certain parents, certain brothers, a certain homeland, a certain rank. And now you come to me and say, 'Let's change the subject.'" *Epict. Diss.*, I, XXIX, 41: "The day will soon

come when actors will believe that they themselves are their mask and costumes."

52. *Epict. Diss.*, I, XXIV, 16–18.

53. Boethius, *The Theological Tractates and "The Consolation of Philosophy,"* trans. H. F. Stewart, E. K. Rand, and S. J. Tester (Cambridge, Mass.: Harvard University Press, 1973), pp. 86–87.

54. "Nam illud quidem manifestum est personae subiectam esse naturam nec praeter naturam personam posse predicari." Ibid., p. 82.

55. Medieval allegory, which has been so often discussed, can best be situated in the context of the passage in which Boethius explains that accidents cannot become persons ("videmus personam in accidentibus non posse constitui: quis enim dicat ullam albedinis vel nigredinis vel magnitudinis esse personam?" Ibid., p. 82).

56. *Purgatorio*, XXX, 63, pp. 330–31.

57. On this thesis, which has its origin in Völkelt, see Walter Benjamin's remarks in *Ursprung des deutschen Trauerspiels*, in Walter Benjamin, *Gesammelte Schriften*, ed. Rolf Tiedemann and Hermann Schweppenhäuser, vol. I, 1 (Frankfurt am Main: Suhrkamp, 1974), pp. 279–80; translated as *The Origin of the German Tragic Drama*, trans. J. Osborne (London: Verso, 1977), pp. 100–102.

58. Dante, *Opere minori*, vol. II, 2, *Convivio*, IV, VI, 20, p. 595; *Dante's "Il Convivio" (The Banquet)*, p. 165: "Better would it be for you to fly low like a sparrow than to soar aloft like a kite over things that are totally base" (*Meglio sarebbe a voi come ronde volare basso, che come nibbio altissime rote fare sopra cose vilissime*).

2. 'Corn:' From Anatomy to Poetics

1. *The Vidas of the Troubadours*, trans. Margarita Egan (New York: Garland, 1984), p. 93. Translation slightly modified.

2. The critical text of Arnaut used here is that edited by Mario Eusebi, *Arnaut Daniel, Il Sirventese e le Canzoni* (Milan: All'insegna del pesce d'oro, 1984) (from which I depart only in writing the name *Ayna*, as opposed to *Ena*).

3. Ugo A. Canello, *La vita e le opere del trovatore Arnaldo Daniello* (Halle: Niemeyer, 1883), p. 187.

4. R. Lavaud, *Les poésies d'Arnaut Daniel: Réedition critique d'après Canello*, in *Annales du Midi* 22 (1910) and 23 (1911) (Geneva: Slatkine Reprints, 1973), p. 9.

5. Gianluigi Toja, *Arnaut Daniel, Canzoni* (Florence: Sansoni, 1960), p. 182.

6. Maurizio Perugi, *Le Canzoni di Arnaut Daniel* (Milan: Ricciardi, 1978), 2: 4–10.

7. L. Lazzerini, "Cornar lo corn: Sulla tenzone tra Raimon de Dufort, Truc Malec and Arnaut Daniel," in *Medioevo romanzo* 8 (1981–83): 339–40.

8. Eusebi, *Arnaut Daniel*, pp. 1–2.

9. Andreas Heusler, *Deutsche Versgeschichte* (Berlin: de Gruyter, 1956), 2: 332.

10. *De vulgari eloquentia*, ed. and trans. Steven Botterill (Cambridge, Eng.: Cambridge University Press, 1996), pp. 84–85.

11. Matthias Lexer, *Mittelhochdeutsches Handwörterbuch* (Stuttgart: Hirzel, 1979), p. 1691.

12. Heusler, *Deutsche Versgeschichte*, p. 331.

13. Maria Careri, *Il Canzoniere provenzale H, Struttura, contenuto e fonti* (Modena: Mucchi, 1990), p. 284.

14. Emil Levy, *Petit dictionnaire provençal-français* (Heidelberg: C. Winter, 1966).

15. Eusebi, *Arnaut Daniel*, p. 9.

16. See two flagrant examples in Pierre Bec, *Burlesque et obscenité chez les troubadours* (Paris: Stock, 1984), pp. 127–30, in particular "Que'm mostrès son conjunctiu."

17. *The Poetry of Arnaut Daniel*, ed. and trans. James J. Wilhelm (New York: Garland, 1981), p. 45.

18. Ibid., p. 3.

19. Eusebi, *Arnaut Daniel*, p. 128.

20. Levy, *Petit dictionnaire provençal-français*, p. 96.

21. Costanzo Di Girolamo, *Elementi di versificazione provenzale* (Naples: Liguori Editore, 1979), p. 116.

22. *De vulgari eloquentia*, II, XIII, 2, pp. 82–85.

23. See the list in Toja, *Arnaut Daniel, Canzoni*, p. 41.

24. Friedrich Diez, *Leben und Werke der Trobadours* (Leipzig: J. A. Barth, 1882), p. 286.

25. *Las Flors del gay saber* (Toulouse: Gatien-Arnout, 1841–43), 3: 330.

26. *The Poetry of Arnaut Daniel*, p. 49.

27. Di Girolamo, *Elementi di versificazione*, p. 41.

28. Gianfranco Contini, *Varianti e altra linguistica* (Turin: Einaudi, 1970), p. 315.

29. Stéphane Mallarmé, *Œuvres complètes* (Paris: Pléiade, 1966), p. 455.

30. Dante Alighieri, *The Divine Comedy, Purgatorio*, trans. Charles S. Singleton (Princeton, N.J.: Princeton University Press, 1973), pp. 18–19.

31. *De vulgari eloquentia*, II, 8, 5–6, pp. 70–71.

32. Guglielmo Gorni, *Il nodo della lingua e il verbo d'amore* (Florence: L. S. Olschki, 1981), p. 41.

33. Di Girolamo, *Elementi di versificazione*, p. 29.

34. Georges Lote, *Histoire du vers français* (Paris: Boivin, 1949), 1: 167–72.

35. "Et devetz saber que nos cossiram pauza en dos manieras, la una cant a la sentensa: e segon aquesta maniera en tot loc del bordo pot estar pauza suspensiva, plena o finals . . . en autra manera cossiram pauza en quant que la prendem por una alenada." *Las Flors del Gai Saber, estier dichas Las Leys d'Amors*, ed. Adolphe F. Gatien-Arnoult, 3 vols. (Toulouse: Typ. de J.-B. Paya, 1841–43), 1: 130.

36. Lote, *Histoire du vers français*, p. 252.

37. *De vulgari eloquentia*, II, IX, 2–3, pp. 72–73. Emphasis mine.

38. Ibid., II, X, 1.

39. Roger Dragonetti, "Dante face à Nemrod: Babel mémoire et miroir de l'Eden," *Critique* 387–388 (1979): 705.

40. Gorni, *Il nodo della lingua*, p. 29.

41. *Dante's "Il Convivio" (The Banquet)*, trans. Richard H. Lansing (New York: Garland, 1990), pp. 95–96. The Italian text reads as follows: "Però che li miei pensieri, di costei ragionando, molte fiate voleano cose conchiudere di lei che io non le oeta intendere, e smarrivami, sì che quasi parea di fuori alienato. . . . E questa è l'una ineffablitade di quello che io per tema ho preso; e conseguentemente narro l'altra . . . e dico che li miei pensieri—che sono parlare d'amore—sonan sì dolci, che la mia anima, cioè lo mio affetto arde di poter ciò con la lingua narrare; e perché dire nol posso . . . questa è l'altra ineffabilitade; cioè che la lingua non è di quello che lo'ntelletto vede compiutamente seguace . . . Dico adunque che la mia insufficenza procede doppiamente, sì come doppiamente trascende l'altezza di costei, per lo modo che detto è. Ché a me conviene lasciare per povertà d'intelletto molto di quello che è vero di lei, e che quasi ne la mia mente raggia, la quale come corpo diafano riceve quello, non terminando: e questo dico in quello seguente particula: *E certo e' mi conven lasciare in pria*. Poi quando dico: *E di quel s'intende*, dico che non pur a quello che lo mio intelletto non sostiene, ma eziando a quello che io intendo sufficiente non sono, però che la lingua mia non è tanta fa-

cundia che dire potesse ciò che nel pensiero mio se ne ragiona." Dante Alighieri, *Opere minori*, II, 1, ed. Cesare Vasoli and Domenico De Robertis (Milan: Ricciardi, 1995), II, 1.

42. *Purgatorio*, pp. 150–51.

43. Ibid., XXVI, 106–8, pp. 284–85.

44. Ibid., XXIV, 61–62, pp. 260–61.

45. Gorni, *Il nodo della lingua*, p. 20.

46. Édouard Jeaneau, *Quatre thèmes érigéniens* (Toronto: Pontifical Institute of Medieaval Studies, 1978), p. 112.

3. The Dream of Language

1. Citations of *Hypnerotomachia Poliphili* refer to the critical edition of Giovanni Pozzi and Lucia A. Ciapponi, 2 vols. (Padova: Editrice Antenori, 1968).

2. Maria Teresa Casella-Pozzi, *Francesco Colonna: Biografia e opere*, 2 vols. (Padova: Editrice Antenori, 1959), 2: 79.

3. A list of these delays and anomalies is given ibid., pp. 117–26, and is expanded in *Hypnerotomachia*, 2: 33–35.

4. I refer to the analysis in K. H. Stierle, "Linguaggio assoluto e linguaggio strumentale in Mallarmé," *Metaphorein* 3 (1978): 17–34.

5. Stéphane Mallarmé, *Selected Prose Poems, Essays, and Letters*, trans. Bradford Cook (Baltimore: The Johns Hopkins University Press, 1956), p. 33.

6. Stéphane Mallarmé, *Œuvres complètes*, ed. Henri Mondor and C. Jean-Aubry (Paris: Pléiade, 1945), p. 386.

7. Hans Wilhelm Klein, *Latein und Volgare in Italien* (Munich: M. Hueber, 1957).

8. Sicco Polenton, *Sicconis Polentoni Scriptorum illustrium latinae linguae libri XVIII*, ed. B. L. Ullmann (Rome: American Academy in Rome, 1928), p. 129.

9. Sperone Speroni, *Dialogo delle lingue e dialogo della rettorica* (Lanciano: R. Carabba, 1912), pp. 54–58.

10. Claudio Tolomei, cited in Klein, *Latein und Volgare*, p. 82.

11. Carlo Dionisotti, "Niccolò Liburnio e la cultura cortigiana," *Letture Italiane* 14 (1962): 38.

12. The English translation of Dante's *Convivio* cited here is that in *Dante's "Il Convivio" (The Banquet)*, trans. Richard H. Lansing (New York: Garland, 1990), p. 31.

13. Ibid., p. 70.

14. Pozzi-Ciapponi's comment in *Hypnerotomachia*, 2: 19.

15. For a discussion of this text, see Ernst Robert Curtius, *European Literature and the Latin Middle Ages*, trans. Willard R. Trask (Princeton, N.J.: Princeton University Press, 1953), pp. 374–78. The translation cited is the one published in this work.

4. Pascoli and the Thought of the Voice

1. "Egli confonde la sua voce con la nostra . . . si sente un palpito solo, uno strillare e un guaire . . . tinnulo squillo come di campanello . . . udirne il chiacchiericcio."

5. The Dictation of Poetry

1. St. Augustine, *De Trinitate*, IX, 10, 15.

2. Dante Alighieri, *The Divine Comedy*, *Purgatorio*, trans. Charles S. Singleton (Princeton, N.J.: Princeton University Press, 1973), XXIV, 58–59, pp. 260–61.

6. Expropriated Manner

1. The timing can be surmised given the letter to Gianni D'Elia, the president of "Lengua," which was sent together with the fourth and definitive draft of the poem.

2. This is the same subject that Kafka, in the years of the Great War, discussed with his friend Felix Weltsch, author of a book entitled *Freedom and Grace*: "Who was Pelagius? I have read many things on Pelagianism, but I do not remember a thing." Letter of Kafka to F. Weltsch, December 1917.

3. "Quamquam inseparabilem habere possibiltatem id est, ut ita dicam, inamissibilem." St. Augustine, *De natura et gratia*, LI, 59.

4. Friedrich Hölderlin, *Sämtliche Werke*, ed. Friedrich Beißner (Stuttgart: W. Kohlhammer, 1953), 2: 388.

5. "Irrespirabile per i più. Dura e incolore come un quarzo. Nera e trasparente (e tagliente) come l'ossidiana. L'allegria ch'essa può dare è indicibile. È l'adito—troncata netta ogni speranza—a tutte le libertà possibili. Compresa quella (la serpe che si morde la coda) di credere in Dio, pur sapendo—definitivamente—che non c'è e non esiste."

6. The observation was made by F. Milana, "Invoca il non invocabile," *Azione sociale* 5 (1990).

7. "Il bene e il male sono due specchi / della stessa illusione: che è quella / di viver padroni dell'essere proprio."

8. Dante Alighieri, *The Divine Comedy, Purgatorio*, trans. Charles S. Singleton (Princeton, N.J.: Princeton University Pres, 1973), XXIV, 52–54, pp. 260–61.

9. According to the felicitous formulation of Cesare Garboli, in Giovanni Pascoli, *Poesie famigliari*, ed. Cesare Garboli (Milan: Mondadori, 1985).

10. Pizzuto's *Paginette* is now reprinted in Gianfranco Contini, *Varianti e altra linguistica* (Turin: Einaudi, 1970), pp. 621–25.

11. "Harsh" and "sweet" techniques are meant here in the strong sense of "polar partition of the lyric style" that these expressions, drawn from Hellenistic rhetoric (*harmonia austera, harmonia glaphyra*), have in Norbert von Hellingrath's commentaries on Hölderlin.

12. The proliferation of internal rhymes in Caproni's poems—which is clearly intentional, as shown by close examination of the manuscripts—is another sign (if ambiguous, like the preceding ones) of this tendency to call into question the unity of the verse (which is already implicit in Mallarmé's attempt to substitute the page, by means of blanks, for the verse as a rhythmic unity).

13. ["Counter-Caproni" is the title given by Caproni to a group of compositions at the end of *Res amissa*, in which the poet parodies his own poems.—*Trans.*]

7. The Celebration of the Hidden Treasure

1. Baruch Spinoza, *Ethics, Treatise on the Emendation of the Intellect and Selected Letters*, trans. Samuel Shirley, ed. Seymour Feldman (Indianapolis: Hackett, 1992), p. 31.

2. Ibid.

3. Ibid., p. 36.

4. Ibid., p. 49.

5. Ibid., p. 174.

6. Ibid., p. 139.

Appendix B: The Hunt for Language

1. Dante Alighieri, *The Divine Comedy, Inferno*, trans. Charles S. Singleton (Princeton, N.J.: Princeton University Press, 1970), pp. 330–33.

Appendix C: The Just Do Not Feed on Light

    1. Paul Celan, *Gedichte in zwei Bänden* (Frankfurt: Surhkamp, 1975), 2: 202.

    2. *Poems of Paul Celan*, trans. Michael Hamburger (New York: Persea Books, 1988), pp. 288–89.

M E R I D I A N

Crossing Aesthetics

Library of Congress Cataloging-in-Publication Data

Agamben, Giorgio
   [Categorie italiane.   English]
   The end of the poem : studies in poetics / Giorgio Agamben ;
translated by Daniel Heller-Roazen.
       p.   cm. — (Meridian, crossing aesthetics)
   Includes bibliographical references.
     ISBN 0-8047-3021-0 (cloth : alk. paper). — ISBN 0-8047-3022-9
(paper : alk. paper)
     1. Italian poetry—History and criticism.   2. Poetics.
I. Heller-Roazen, Daniel.   II. Title.   III. Series: Meridian
(Stanford, Calif.)
PQ4093.A3513   1999
851.009—dc21   99-22592

⊗   This book is printed on acid-free, recycled paper.

Original printing 1999
Last figure below indicates year of this printing:
08   07   06   05   04